Praise for *A Thousand*

"You will be swept away, enchanted by the story, and revel in the details of this intimate celebration of a man, a woman, and Italy."

—Adriana Trigiani, author of *Big Stone Gap*

"The story sounds impossibly romantic . . . [But] this moonstruck tale is absolutely true . . . It is, surprisingly, a story with a happy ending—reached, as real-life happy endings must be, not by fiat but by accommodation." —*The Boston Globe*

"A true, disarming, and unexpectedly endearing romance. This is passionate romance at its best, not the idealistic hero and heroine, nor their lusts, but the comedy and tenderness of two lives joined together rather belatedly." —*Chicago Sun Times*

"Is this book a romance, a food guide, or an exhortation for us to come to Venice and experience the magic? Ultimately, it is all three." —*Library Journal*

"*A Thousand Days in Venice* is a little cioppino of a book, a tasty stew with equal parts travel and food and romance, spiced up with goodly amounts of fantasy-come-true . . . An appealing tale of a true romance and a second chance." —*The Seattle Post-Intelligencer*

"An irresistible grown-up love story." —*USA Today*

# A Thousand Days in Venice

# A Thousand Days in Venice

## AN UNEXPECTED ROMANCE

### by Marlena de Blasi

Algonquin Books of Chapel Hill    2013

Published by

ALGONQUIN BOOKS OF CHAPEL HILL

Post Office Box 2225

Chapel Hill, North Carolina 27515-2225

a division of

Workman Publishing

225 Varick Street

New York, New York 10014

Library of Congress Cataloging-in-Publication Data

De Blasi, Marlena.

   A thousand days in Venice : an unexpected romance / by Marlena de Blasi.

   p. cm.

ISBN 978-1-56512-321-2 (HC)

   1. Venice (Italy)—Description and travel.   2. Venice (Italy)—Social life and customs.
3. De Blasi, Marlena—Homes and haunts—Italy—Venice.   I. Title.

DG674.2 .D35 2002

945'.31—dc21                                                                      2002018305

ISBN 978-1-61620-281-1 (PB)

10   9   8   7   6   5   4   3   2   1

FOR

WALTON AMOS'S BABY GIRL, VIRGINIA ANDERSON AMOS,

WHO GREW UP TO BE A BEAUTIFUL WOMAN FULL OF GOD'S

GRACE AND LOVE WHOM I AM HONORED TO CALL

MY DARLING FRIEND

AND

FOR C. D., LISA, AND ERICH,

MY FIRST AND FOREVER LOVES

AND

FOR THE BLUEBERRY-EYED VENETIAN WHO WAITED

AND

TO MARGE AND BOB FEDER,

IDEALS, IDOLS, TWO OF THE THIRTY-SIX

# Contents

# A Thousand Days in Venice

# Prologue

## VENICE, 1989

*I* sit in my seat long after the train swooshes into its berth at Santa
Lucia. I paint a fresh coat of ruby red on my lips, pull a blue felt
cloche down to my eyebrows and try to smooth my skirt. I think for a moment
of the tale I'd told the taxi driver in Rome earlier that morning. He'd asked,
"Ma dove vai in questo giorno cosí splendido? *But where are you going on this splendid day?*"

"*I have a rendezvous in Venice,*" *I'd said slyly, knowing the image would
please him.*

*Watching as I'd pulled my fat, black suitcase with its one crumpled wheel
backward into the curve of the station doors, he'd blown me a kiss and yelled,*
"Porta un mio abbraccio a la bella Venezia. *Carry an embrace from me
to beautiful Venice.*"

*Even a Roman taxi driver is in love with Venice! Everyone's in love with
her. Everyone except me. I've never been to Venice, having always been indif-
ferent about wandering through all those iridescent torpors of hers. Still perhaps what I'd told the taxi driver is true. I am behaving curiously like a
woman on her way to a rendezvous. Now that I'm finally here, though, I wish
I could spurn the Old Woman of Byzantium once again.*

*Exiting the now empty train, I tug my suitcase down onto the platform,
giving its evil wheel a kick for encouragement, and stride through the tumult
of the station, amidst vendors peddling water taxis and hotels, travelers in the
anguishes of arrival and departure. The doors are open and I step out into
wet rosy light, onto a sweep of wide shallow steps. Shimmering water glints*

*from the canal below. I don't know where to put my eyes. The Venice of myth is real, rolled out before me. In straw hats and striped shirts, the gondolieri are sculptures of themselves fixed on the sterns of glossy black boats under a round yellow sun. The Bridge of the Barefoot is off to the left and the sweet façade of the church of San Simeone Piccolo hails from across the water. All of Venice is tattered, resewn, achingly lovely, and like an enchantress, she disarms me, makes off with the very breath of me.*

*I wait for the* vaporetto, *the water bus, line number 1, and embark on a boat that moves,* pian, piano *up the canal, stopping fourteen times between the station and San Zaccaria near the Piazza San Marco. I stow my bag in the great heap of luggage on the deck and make my way out onto the prow, hoping to stay outdoors. The benches are occupied, except a few inches where a Japanese woman's purse sits. I smile, she moves her Fendi, and I ride amid crisp winds up the astonishing highway. Strange now to think that this boat was to become my habitual transport, this water my daily route from home to buy lettuces, to find a wedding dress, to go to the dentist, to light a candle in a thousand-year-old church.*

*Along the* riva *totter the palaces, fragile Byzantine and Gothic faces, the Renaissance, the baroque all in a melancholic row, each one leaning fast against the next. The better to stifle secrets I think. As we approach the Ponte di Rialto, the exit nearest my hotel, I am not ready to leave the boat. I stay on through to San Zaccaria and walk off the landing stage toward the* campanile, *the bell tower. I wait for a moment, listening for the clanging of la Marangona, the most ancient of San Marco's bells, the one whose solemn basso has signaled the beginning and the end of the Venetian artisan's workday for fifteen centuries. Once it warned of enemy approach, saluted a visiting king, and announced the death of a doge. Some say it rings by its own will, that if one arrives in Venice to its great, noble clanging, it is proof of* one's Venetian soul, proof the old bell remembers one from some other time. When a friend first told me this story years ago, I asked him how, if six hundred people were passing by at any given moment, anyone would know for whom the bell was ringing. "Don't worry," he said. "It will never ring for you."

La Marangona is, indeed, silent as I stand before the tower. I don't look at the basilica sitting there behind my shoulders. I don't walk the few meters into the grand piazza. I'm not ready. Not ready for what? I tell myself it's only that one can't wander into what is touted as the earth's most divine drawing room, bedraggled, shackled by a rickety suitcase. I turn back, take the next boat going toward the station, and debark at Rialto. Why is my heart flailing against my chest? Even as I am now drawn to Venice, so am I suspicious of her.

# I

# Signora, the Telephone Is for You

*T*he small room is filled with German tourists, a few English, and a table or two of locals. It's November 6, 1993, and I arrived in Venice that morning, two friends in tow. We speak quietly together, sipping Amarone. Time passes and the room empties, but I notice that one table, the one farthest away from us, remains occupied. I feel the gentle, noninvasive stare of one of the four men who sit there. I turn my shoulders in, toward my wine, never really looking at the man. Soon the gentlemen go off, and we three are alone in the place. A few minutes pass before a waiter comes by to say there is a telephone call for me. We have yet to announce our arrival to friends, and even if someone knew we were in Venice, they couldn't possibly know we were lunching at Vino Vino. I tell the waiter he's mistaken. "No, signora. Il telefono è per Lei," he insists.

*"Pronto,"* I say into the old, orange wall telephone that smells of smoke and men's cologne.

*"Pronto.* Is it possible for you to meet me tomorrow at the same time? It's very important for me," says a deep, deliberate, Italian voice I'd never heard before.

In the short silence that follows it somehow clicks that he is one of the men who'd left the restaurant just moments before. Though

I've understood fairly well what he has said, I can't respond in Italian. I mumble some linguistic fusion like, *"No, grazie.* I don't even know who you are," thinking that I really like his voice.

The next day we decide to return to Vino Vino because of its convenience to our hotel. I don't think about the man with the beautiful voice. But he's there, and this time he's without his colleagues and looking more than a little like Peter Sellers. We smile. I go off to sit with my friends, and he, seeming not quite to know how to approach us, turns and goes out the door. A few beats pass before the same waiter, now feeling a part of something quite grand, comes to me, eyes direct: *"Signora, il telefono è per Lei."* There ensues a repeat of yesterday's scene.

I go to the phone, and the beautiful voice speaks in very studied English, perhaps thinking it was his language I hadn't understood the day before: "Is it possible for you to meet me tomorrow, alone?"

"I don't think so," I fumble, "I think I'm going to Naples."

"Oh," is all the beautiful voice can say.

"I'm sorry," I say and hang up the phone.

We don't go to Naples the next day or the day after, but we do go to the same place for lunch, and Peter Sellers is always there. We never speak a word face to face. He always telephones. And I always tell him I can't meet him. On the fifth day—a Friday—our last full day in Venice, my friends and I spend the morning at Florian mapping the rest of our journey, drinking Prosecco and cups of bitter, thick chocolate lit with Grand Marnier. We decide not to have lunch but to save our appetites for a farewell dinner at Harry's Bar. Walking back to the hotel, we pass by Vino Vino, and there is Peter Sellers, his nose pressed against the window. A lost child. We stop in the *calle* a moment, and my friend Silvia says, "Go inside and talk to him. He has the dearest face. We'll meet you at the hotel."

I sit down next to the sweet face with the beautiful voice, and we drink some wine. We talk very little, something about the rain, I think, and why I didn't come to lunch that day. He tells me he is the manager of a nearby branch of Banca Commerciale Italiana, that it's late, and he has the only set of keys to reopen the safe for the afternoon's business. I notice the sweet face with the beautiful voice has wonderful hands. His hands tremble as he gathers his things to leave. We agree to meet at six-thirty that evening, right there, in the same place. *"Proprio qui,* Right here," he repeats again and again.

I walk to the hotel with a peculiar feeling and spend the afternoon lolling about my little room, only half celebrating my tradition of reading Thomas Mann in bed. Even after all these years of coming to Venice, every afternoon is a ritual. Close by on the night table I place some luscious little pastry or a few cookies or, if lunch was too light, maybe one, crusty *panino* which Lino at the *bottega* across the bridge from my Pensione Accademia has split and stuffed with prosciutto, then wrapped in butcher's paper. I tuck the down quilt under my arms and open my book. But today I read and don't read the same page for an hour. And the second part of the ritual falls away altogether, the part where I wander out to see images Mann saw, touch stones he touched. Today all I can think about is *him.*

The persevering rain becomes a tempest that night, but I am resolved to meet the stranger. Lagoon waters splash up and spill over onto the *riva* in great foaming pools and the Piazza is a lake of black water. The winds seem the breath of furies. I make my way to the warm safety of the bar at the Hotel Monaco but no farther. Less than a few hundred yards from Vino Vino, I'm so close but I can get no closer. I go to the desk and ask for a telephone directory, but the wine bar is not listed. I try calling *assistenza* but operator number 143 finds nothing. The rendezvous is a wreckage, and I haven't a way to contact Peter Sellers. It was just not meant to be. I head back to the hotel bar, where a waiter called Paolo stuffs my soaked boots with newspaper and places them near a radiator with the same ceremony someone else might use to stow the crown jewels. I've known Paolo since my first trip to Venice four years earlier. Stocking-footed, fidgeting, drinking tea, I sit on the damp layers of my skirt, which sends up the wooly perfume of wet lambs, and watch fierce, crackling lights rip the clouds. I think back to my very first time in Venice. Lord, how I fought that journey! I'd been in Rome for a few days, and I'd wanted to stay. But there I was, hunkered down in a second-class train, heading north.

*"Are you going to Venice?" asks a small voice in tentative Italian, trespassing on my Roman half-dream.*

*I open my eyes and look out the window to see we have pulled into Tiburtina. Two young, pink-faced German women are hoisting their great packs up into the overhead space, thrusting their ample selves down onto the seat opposite me.*

*"Yes," I finally answer, in English, to a space somewhere between them. "For the first time," I say.*

*They are serious, shy, dutifully reading the Lorenzetti guide to Venice and drinking mineral water in the hot, airless train car as it lunges and bumps over the flat Roman countryside and up into the Umbrian hills. I close my eyes again, trying to find my place in the fable of life in the Via Giulia where*

*I'd taken roof-top rooms in the ochered-rose palazzo that sits across from the Hungarian Art Academy. I'd decided I would go each Friday to eat a bowlful of tripe at Da Felice in the Testaccio. I would shop every morning in Campo dei Fiori. I'd open a twenty-seat* taverna *in the Ghetto, one big table where the shopkeeps and artisans would come to eat the good food I'd cook for them. I'd take a Corsican prince as my lover. His skin would smell of neroli blossoms, and he'd be poor as I would be, and we'd walk along the Tiber, going softly into our dotage. As I begin putting together the exquisite pieces of the prince's face, the trespasser's small voice asks, "Why are you going to Venice? Do you have friends there?"*

*"No. No friends," I tell her. "I guess I'm going because I've never been there, because I think I should," I say, more to myself than to her. I have hopelessly lost the prince's face for the moment, and so I parry: "And why are you going to Venice?"*

*"For romance," says the inquisitive one very simply.*

*My plainer truth is that I am going to Venice because I'm being sent there, to gather notes for a series of articles. Twenty-five hundred words on the* bacari, *traditional Venetian wine bars; twenty-five hundred more on the question of the city's gradual sinking into the lagoon; and an upscale dining review. I would rather have stayed in Rome. I want to go back to my narrow green wooden bed in the strange little room tucked up in the fourth-floor eaves of the Hotel Adriano. I want to sleep there, to be awakened by powdery sunlight sifting in through the chinks in the shutters. I like the way my heart beats in Rome, how I can walk faster and see better. I like that I feel at home wandering through her ancient ecstasy of secrets and lies. I like that she's taught me I am only a scintilla, a barely perceptible and transient gleam. And I like that at lunch, with fried artichokes on my breath, I think of supper. And at supper I remember peaches that wait in a bowl of cool water near my bed. I've nearly retrieved the pieces of the prince's face as the train lurches over the Ponte della Libertà. I open my eyes to see the lagoon.*

BACK THEN I COULD never have imagined how sweetly this ravishing old Princess was to gather me up into her tribe, how she would dazzle and dance the way only she can, exploding a morning with gold-shot light, soaking an evening in the bluish mists of a trance. I smile at Paolo, a tribal smile, a soundless eloquence. He stays near, keeping my teapot full.

It's after eleven-thirty before the storm rests. I pull on boots all hardened into the shape of the newsprint stuffing. Damp hat over still-damp hair, still-damp coat, I gather myself for the walk back to the hotel. Something prickles, shivers forward in my consciousness. I try to remember if I'd told the stranger where we were staying. What's happening to me? Me, the unflappable. *Even as I am drawn to Venice, so am I suspicious of her.*

It seems I *did* tell him the name of our hotel, because I find a sheaf of pink paper messages under my door. He'd called every half hour from seven until midnight, the last message letting me know he would be waiting in the lobby at noon the next day, exactly the hour we were to leave for the airport.

Morning brings the first sun we've seen in Venice during that stay. I heave open my window to a day limpid and soft, as if in apology for all that weeping the night before. I pull on black velvet leggings and a turtleneck and go down to meet Peter Sellers, to look him in the eyes and to find out why a man I'd hardly met could be so disturbing to me. I don't know how I'm going to find out very much though, because he seems to speak no English and the only clear discourse I can carry on in Italian is about food. I'm a bit early, so I walk outside to feel the air and find I'm just in time to see him climbing over the *Ponte delle Maravegie,* trench coat, cigarette, newspaper, umbrella. I see him before he sees me. And I like what I see, feel.

"*Stai scappando?* Are you escaping?" he asks.

"No. I was coming to meet you," I say, mostly with my hands.

I had told my friends to wait, that I'd be half an hour, an hour at most. We would still have plenty of time to take a water taxi to the Marco Polo airport and check in for our three o'clock flight to Naples. I look at him. I really look at the stranger for the first time. All I see is the blue of his eyes. They are colored like the sky and the water are colored today and like the tiny, purply-blue berries called *mirtilli,* I think. He is at once shy and familiar, and we walk without destination. We stop for a moment on the Ponte dell'Accademia. He keeps dropping his newspaper and, as he bends to retrieve it, he thrusts the point of his umbrella into the crowds that pass behind us. Then, holding the newspaper under one arm and the umbrella under the other, its evil point still a thwart to the strollers, he slaps at his breast pockets, his trouser pockets, in search of a match. He finds the match and then begins the same search for another cigarette to replace the one that just dropped from his lips into the canal. He really is Peter Sellers.

He asks if I've ever thought much about destiny and if I believe there is such a thing as *vero amore,* real love. He looks away from me out over the water and speaks in a throaty sort of stammer for what seems like a long time and more to himself than to me. I understand few of the words except his final phrase, *una volta nella vita,* once in a lifetime. He looks at me as though he wants to kiss me, and I think

I'd like to kiss him, too, but I know the umbrella and the newspaper will go into the water and, besides, we're too old to be playing love scenes. Aren't we too old? I'd probably want to kiss him even if he didn't have blueberry eyes. I'd probably want to kiss him even if he looked like Ted Koppel. It's only this place, the view from this bridge, this air, this light. I wonder if I'd want to kiss him if I'd met him in Naples. We take a gelato at Paolin in Campo Santo Stefano, sitting down at a front-row table in the sun.

"How do you feel about Venice?," he wants to know. "This is not your first visit here," he says, as though flipping through some internal dossier that tracks all my European movement.

"No, no, this is not my first time. I began coming in the spring of '89, about four years ago," I tell him brightly.

"1989? You've been coming to Venice for four years?" he asks. He holds up four fingers as though my pronounciation of *quattro* was muddled.

"Yes," I say. "Why is that so strange?"

"It's only that I never saw you until December. Last December. December 11, 1992," he says, as though eyeing the dossier more closely.

"What?" I ask, a little stunned, rummaging back to last winter, computing the dates when I'd last been there. Yes, I'd arrived in Venice on December 2 and then flown up to Milan on the evening of the eleventh. Still, he's surely mistaken me for another woman, and I'm about to tell him that, but he's already lunging into his story.

"You were walking in Piazza San Marco; it was just after five in the afternoon. You were wearing a long white coat, very long, down to your ankles, and your hair was tied up, just as it is now. You were looking in the window at Missiaglia, and you were with a man. He wasn't Venetian, or at least I'd never seen him before. Who was he?" he asks stiffly.

Before I can push out half a syllable, he is asking, "Was he your lover?"

I know he doesn't want me to answer, and so I don't. He's talking faster now, and I'm losing words and phrases. I ask him to look at me and, please, to speak more slowly. He accommodates. "I saw you only in profile, and I kept walking toward you. I stopped a few feet from you, and I just stood still, taking you in. I stood there until you and the man walked off the piazza toward the quay." He illustrates his words with broad movements of his hands, his fingers. His eyes hold mine urgently.

"I began to follow you, but I stopped because I had no idea what I'd do if I came face to face with you. I mean what would I say to you? How could I find a way to talk to you? And so I let you go. That's what I do, you know, I just let things go. I looked for you the next day and the next, but I knew you were gone. If only I'd see you walking alone somewhere, I could stop you, pretending I mistook you for someone else. No, I would tell you I thought your coat was beautiful. But anyway, I never found you again, so I held you in my mind. For all these months I tried to imagine who you were, where you were from. I wanted to hear the sound of your voice. I was very jealous of the man with you," he says slowly. "And then, as I was sitting there at Vino Vino the other day and you angled your body so that your profile was just visible underneath all that hair, I realized it was you. The woman in the white coat. And so you see, I've been waiting for you. Somehow I've been loving you, *loving* you since that afternoon in the piazza."

Still I have said not a word.

"That's what I was trying to tell you on the bridge just now, about destiny and true love. I fell in love with you, not at first sight, because I saw only a part of your face. With me it was love at half sight. It was enough. And if you think I'm mad, I don't care."

~

"Is it okay if I speak?" I ask him very quietly and without a notion of what I want to tell him. His eyes are now deep blue bolts, holding me much too tightly. I look down, and when I look up again his eyes have softened. I hear myself saying, "It's a very sweet gift, this telling of your story. But that you saw me and remembered me and then that you saw me again a year later is not so mysterious an event. Venice is a very small city, and it is not improbable to see the same people again and again. I don't think our meeting is some sort of thundering stroke of destiny. Anyway how can you be in love with a *profile?* I'm not only a *profile;* I'm thighs and elbows and brain. I'm a woman. I think all of this is only coincidence, a very touching coincidence," I say to the blueberry eyes, neatly patting his arcadian testimony into smooth shape as I might a heft of bread dough.

*"Non è una coincidenza.* This is not coincidence. I'm in love with you, and I'm sorry if this fact makes you uncomfortable."

"It's not discomfort I feel. It's only that I don't understand it. Yet." I say this, wanting to pull him close, wanting to push him away.

"Don't go today. Stay a little longer. Stay with me," he says.

"If there's to be something, anything at all between us, my going today won't change it. We can write to each other, talk. I'll be coming back in the spring, and we can make plans." There seems a forced syncopation to my words before I hear them falling away into near paralysis. Still as a frieze, we sit there on the edges of the *campo*'s Saturday fracas. A long time passes through our silence before we shuffle to our feet. Not waiting for a check, he leaves lire on the table under the glass dish of his untasted strawberry gelato, rivulets of which drip onto the paper money.

My face is burning, and I feel startled, flush up against an emotion I can't name, one eerily like terror but not unlike joy. Could there have been some gist to my old Venetian forebodings? Have the presentiments spun out into the form of this man? Is this *the* rendez-vous? I am drawn to the stranger. I am suspicious of the stranger. *Even as I am drawn to Venice, so am I suspicious of her.* Are he and Venice the same thing? Could he be my Corsican prince masquerading as a bank manager? Why can't Destiny announce itself, be a twelve-headed ass, wear purple trousers, a name tag, even? All I know is that I don't fall in love, neither at first sight nor at half-sight, neither easily nor over time. My heart is rusty from the old pinions that hold it shut. That's what I believe about myself.

We stroll through Campo Manin to San Luca, just making small talk. I stop in mid-stride. He stops, too, and he wraps me up in his arms. He holds me. I hold him.

When we exit from the Bacino Orseolo into San Marco, la Marangona is ringing five bells. It's him, I think. He's the twelve-headed ass in the purple trousers! He's Destiny and the bells only recognize me when I'm with him. No, that's rot. Menopausal gibberish.

Five hours have passed since I left the hotel. I call my friends who are still waiting there, and I vow to meet them and my baggage directly at the airport. The last flight to Naples is at seven-twenty. The Grand Canal is improbably empty, free of the usual tangle of skiffs and gondolas and *sandoli,* permitting the *tassista* to race his water taxi, lurching it, slamming it down brutally onto the water. Peter Sellers and I stand outside in the wind and ride into a lowering, dark red sun. I pull a silver flask from my purse and a tiny, thin glass from a velvet pouch. I pour out cognac and we sip together. Again, he looks as if he's going to kiss me, and this time he does—temples, eyelids, before he finds my mouth. We're not too old.

We exchange numbers and business cards and addresses, having no more powerful amulets. He asks if he might join us later in the week wherever we might be. It isn't a good idea, I tell him. As best I know it, I give him our itinerary so we might be able to say good morning or good evening once in a while. He asks when I'll be returning home, and I tell him.

## 2

# There's a Venetian in My Bed

*E*ighteen days later, and only two after I'd set down again in the United States, Fernando arrives in Saint Louis, his first-ever journey to America. Trembling, pale as ashes, he walks through the gate. He'd missed his connection at JFK, racing not fast enough over a space wider than the Lido, the island off Venice where he lives. The flight had been by far the longest period he'd suffered without a cigarette since he was ten years old. He takes the flowers I hold out to him, and we go home together as though we always had, always would.

Coat and hat and gloves and muffler still in place, he moves softly through the house as though trying to recognize something. Startled that the Sub-Zero is a refrigerator, he opens one of its door expecting to find a clothes closet. "Ma è grandissimo," he marvels.

"Are you hungry?" I ask him, beginning to rattle about in the kitchen. He eyes a small basket of tagliatelle I'd rolled and cut that afternoon.

"Do you have fresh pasta also in America?" he asks, as though that fact would be akin to finding a pyramid in Kentucky.

I start the bath for him, as I would for my child or an old lover, pour in sandlewood oil, light candles, place towels and soaps and shampoo on a table nearby. I set down a tiny glass of Tio Pepe. After an alarmingly long passage of time, he saunters into the living room, splendid, wet hair slicked back flat. He wears a vintage dark green woolen robe, one of whose pockets is torn and bulging with a package of cigarettes. Burgundy argyle socks are hiked up over his thin knees, his feet tucked into big, suede slippers. I tell him he looks like Rudolf Valentino. He likes this. I've set our places on the low table in front of the living-room fire. I hand him a glass of red wine, and we sit on cushions. He likes this, too. And so I have supper with the stranger.

There is a white oval dish of braised leeks tossed in crème fraîche, spritzed with vodka, bubbling, golden under a crust of Emmenthaler and Parmesan. I don't know how to say "leek" in Italian, and so I have to get up to find my dictionary. "Ah, *porri*," he says. "I don't like *porri*." I quickly rifle the pages again, pretending to have made an error.

"No, they're not *porri;* these are *scalogni*," I lie to the stranger.

"I've never tasted them," he says, taking a bite. As it turns out, the stranger very much likes leeks, as long as they are called shallots. Then there are the tagliatelle, thin yellow ribbons in a roasted walnut sauce. We are comfortable, uncomfortable. We smile more than we talk. I try to tell him a little about my work, that I'm a journalist, that I write mostly about food and wine. I tell him I'm a chef. He nods indulgently but appears to find my credentials less than compelling. He seems content with silence. I've made a dessert, one I haven't made in years, a funny-looking cake made from bread dough, purple plums, and brown sugar. The thick black juices of the fruit, mingled with the caramelized sugar, give up a fine treacly steam, and we put the cake between us, eating it from the battered old pan I baked it in. He spoons up the last of the plummy syrup, and we drink the heel of the red wine. He gets up and comes over to my side of the table. He sits next to me, looks at me full face, then gently turns my face a bit to the right, holding my chin in his hand. *"Si, questa è la mia faccia,"* he tells me in a whisper. "Yes, this is my face. And I desire now to go with you to your bed." He pronounces these words slowly, clearly, as though he's practiced them.

When he sleeps it's with his cheek against my shoulder, an arm anchoring my waist. I lay awake, stroking his hair. There's a Venetian in my bed, I say almost audibly. I press my mouth to the top of his head and remember again that brusquely delivered assignment I'd received so many years before from my editor: "Spend two weeks in Venice and come back with three feature pieces. We'll send a photographer up from Rome," she'd said, without any good-bye. Why didn't we find each other on that first trip? Probably because my editor never told me to come back with a Venetian. Here he sleeps, though, a stranger with long, skinny legs. But now I must sleep, too. Sleep, I tell myself. But I don't sleep. How can I sleep? I remember the sort of ranging aloofness I'd always suffered about Venice. I'd always found a way to put her off. Once I traveled nearly to the edges of her watery skirts, jaunting over the autostrada from Bergamo to Verona to Padova when, only twenty miles away, I turned my little white Fiat abruptly south toward Bologna. Yet, after the old jaundice about her had been cured during my first Venetian hours, I'd always dug deeply for reasons to return, begging for writing assignments that might take me anywhere close by, trolling the travel sections for the right, cheap ticket.

I moved to Saint Louis, Missouri, last spring from California, staying in a rented room for two months while house renovations were completed and a little café was launched. By June life had shape: the café, a weekly restaurant review for the *Riverfront Times,* the carving out of a day-by-day route through my new city. Still, wanderlust came flirting. Restless by the first days of November, I'd set off with my friends Silvia and Harold, heading back into Venice's honeyed arms. I never thought I'd be heading for *these* honeyed arms, I think as I press closer to the Venetian.

⸻

Mornings, we take to sitting by the kitchen fire, facing each other in the rusty velvet wingback chairs, each with a dual-language dictionary in hand, a full, steaming coffee press, a tiny pitcher of cream, and a plate of buttered scones on the table in front of us. So settled, we speak of our lives.

"I keep trying to remember important things to tell you. You know, about my childhood, about when I was young. I think I am the prototype for Everyman. In the films I would be cast as the man who didn't get the girl." He is neither sad nor apologetic for his self-image.

One morning he wants to know, "Can you remember your dreams?"

"You mean my night dreams?"

"No. Your daydreams. What you thought you wanted? Who you thought you'd be?" he says.

"Of course I can. I've lived many of them. I wanted to have babies. That was my first big one. After they were born, most of my dreams were about them. And when they grew older, I began to dream a little differently. But I really have lived out so many of dreams. I'm living them now. I remember the ones that went up in smoke. I remember all of them, and I've always got new ones rolling around. And you?"

"No. Not so much. And until now, always less. I grew up thinking that dreaming was a lot like sinning. The discourses of my childhood from priests and teachers, from my father, they were about logic, reason, morality, honor. I wanted to fly airplanes and play the saxophone. I went away to school when I was twelve, and, believe me, living among Jesuits does little to encourage dreaming. When I went home, which wasn't very often, things were somber there as well. Youth and, especially, adolescence were offensive stages through which almost everyone tried to rush me."

He is speaking very quickly, and I keep having to ask him to slow down, to explain this word, that word. I'm still back with the Jesuits and the saxophone while he's already onto *la mia adolescenza è stata veramente triste e dura.*

He thinks volume is the solution to my blurred comprehension, and so now he inhales like an aging tenor and his voice swells into thunder. "My father's wish was that I would be quickly *sistemato,* situated, find a job, find a safe path and stay dutifully on it. Early on I learned to want what he wanted. And with time I accumulated layers and layers of barely transparent bandaging over my eyes, over my dreams."

"Wait," I plead, flipping pages, trying to find *cerotti,* bandages. "What happened to your eyes? Why were they in bandages?" I want to know.

*"Non letteralmente.* Not literally," he roars. He is impatient. I am a dolt who, after twelve hours of living with an Italian, cannot yet

follow the drift of his galloping imagery. He adds a third dimension to bring home his story. He's on his feet. Pulling his socks up over wrinkled knees, arranging his robe, now he is wrapping a kitchen towel around his eyes, peeking out over its edge. The stranger has combined speed and volume with histrionics. Surely that will do it. He continues. "And with yet more time, the weight of the bandages, their encumbrance, became hardly noticeable. Sometimes I would squint and look out under the gauze to see if I could still catch a glimpse of the old dreams in real light. Sometimes I could see them. Mostly it would be more comfortable to just go back under the bandages. That is, until now," he says quietly, the show finished.

Maybe he's the man who didn't get the girl unless the girl was Tess of the d'Urbervilles or Anna Karenina. Or, perhaps, Edith Piaf, I think. He's so deeply sad, I think again. And he always wants to talk about "time."

When I ask him why he came racing so quickly across the sea, he tells me he was tired of waiting.

"Tired of waiting? You arrived here two days after I came home," I remind him.

"No. I mean tired of *waiting*. I understand now about using up my time. Life is this *conto*, account," said the banker in him. "It's an unknown quantity of days from which one is permitted to withdraw only one precious one of them at a time. No deposits accepted." This allegory presents glittering opportunity for more of the stranger's stage work. "I've used so many of mine to sleep. One by one, I've mostly waited for them to pass. It's common enough for one to simply find a safe place to wait it all out. Every time I would begin to examine things, to think about what I felt, what I wanted, nothing touched, nothing mattered more than anything else. I've been lazy. Life rolled itself out and I shambled along *sempre due passi indietro,* always two steps behind. *Fatalità,* fate. Easy. No risks. Everything is someone else's fault or merit. And so now, no more waiting," he says as though he's talking to someone far away off in the wings.

When it's my turn, I begin to tell him of some milestone or another—when we moved from New York to California, stories about my brief, terrible stint at the Culinary Institute of America in Hyde Park, about traveling on my stomach to the remotest parts of France and Italy to find one perfect food or wine. Everything sounds like a case history, and after a short roster of recitals I know that none of it matters in the now, that everything I'd done and been until this minute was preamble. Even in these first days together, it is very clear that this feeling of mine for the stranger has trumped all the other adventures in my life. It has shuffled everything and everyone else I thought I was moving toward or away from. Loving Fernando is like a single, sharp shake of the stones that lets me read all the patterns that once baffled and sometimes tortured me. I don't pretend to understand these feelings, but I'm willing to let the inexplicable sit sacred. It seems I had my own set of heirloom bandages. Astonishing what a man bearing tenderness can do to open a heart.

He comes to the café with me each morning, helps with the second bake, chopping rosemary and dumping flour into the Hobart. He loves pulling the focaccia out of the oven on the wooden peel, learning to shake the hot, flat bread deftly onto the cooling racks. We always pat out a small one just for us, set it to bake in the place where the oven's hottest so it comes out brown as hazelnuts. We tear at it impatiently, eating it still steaming, burning our fingers. He says he loves my skin when it smells of rosemary and new bread.

Afternoons we stop in at the newspaper office if I have a column to drop off or something to work out with my editor. We walk in Forest Park. We have supper at the café or go to Balaban's or Café Zoe and then downtown to the jazz clubs. He doesn't understand much about geography, and it's three days before he can be convinced that Saint Louis is in Missouri. He says now he understands why the travel agent in Venice was exasperated when he tried to book a ticket for Saint Louis, Montana. Still, he suggests we go to the Grand Canyon for a day, to New Orleans for lunch.

One evening we return late from dinner at Zoe. We had talked for a long time about life when my children were little. I take a small green faille box of photos from my desk, looking for one to show him of the Lane Gate Road house in Cold Spring, New York, that we all loved so much. Sitting by the fire, the stranger sifts through old vignettes. I join him, and I see he keeps turning back to one of the just-born Lisa, who is cradled in my arms. He says her face is so sweet and so like the face in her grown-up photos, so like her woman's face. He tells me that my face is sweet, too, that Lisa and I look very much alike. He tells me he wishes he'd known me then, wishes he could touch the face that was mine in that old photo.

Now the stranger begins unfastening my bustier, and his hands are beautiful, big, and warm, fumbling as they graze my skin through the soft lace. He begins brushing away crumbs from my décolleté, from between my breasts. *"Cos'è questo?* What is this? Your whole day is recorded here. We have evidence of burnt rye toast; two, perhaps three, kinds of cookies; focaccia; a mocha brownie—it's all here archived inside your lingerie," he says tasting the few telltale bits. I laugh until I cry, and he says, "And about those tears. How many times a day do you cry? Will you always be full of *lacrime e bricole,* full of tears and crumbs?" He presses me down into the cool plush of my bed and, when he kisses me, I taste my own tears mixed with the barest traces of ginger.

"Will you always be full of tears and crumbs?" He's a wise old man, I think, remembering his question while I watch him sleep. Yes, crumbs are the eternal symbol of my intemperate nibbling, my chest forming a good shelf to collect them. And, too, there's some constancy about the tears. Quick to cry as I am to smile, who can tell me why? A long-ago something that still rasps inside me. Something in the pith of me. These are not the stinging, weeping, nighttime tears I can still cry from old wounds. "Stand up you who have nothing left of your wounds," said my friend Misha one evening after a double vodka. After one of his patients shot himself dead with a pearl-handled pistol.

Much of my crying is for joy and wonder rather than for pain. A trumpet's wailing, a wind's warm breath, the chink of a bell on an errant lamb, the smoke from a candle just spent, first light, twilight, firelight. Everyday beauty. I cry for how life intoxicates. And maybe just a little for how swiftly it runs.

∽

Less than a week passes before I awake one morning with a raging flu. I never get flu. It's been years since I've had even a cold, and so now, exactly now, with this Venetian lying in my rosy silk bed, I am burning with fever, my throat is on fire, and I can't breathe for the hundred-pound stone on my chest. I'm beginning to cough. I try to remember what I have in the medicine cabinet for comfort, but I know there is only vitamin C and a ten-year-old, oily, unlabeled bottle of Save-the-Baby that I've carried about since New York.

"Fernando, Fernando," I croak out from the blistery narrows in my throat. "I think I have a fever." At this point I do not yet understand that the word, the concept of "fever," conjures *plague* in the soul of every Italian. I think this phenomenon is a manifestation of medieval memory. Where there is fever, there is sure to be a slow and festering death. He leaps from the bed, repeating "febbre, febbre" and then leaps back into the bed, placing his hands on my forehead and face. He says the word "febbre" at three-second intervals like a mantra. He places his still-hot-from-sleep cheek on my chest and speeds up the mantra. He says my heart is beating very fast and that this is a grave sign. He wants to know the whereabouts of the thermometer, and when I tell him I don't have one I see, for the first time, Fernando's face in torment. I ask him if this thermometer-lessness is a deal breaker.

Not bothering with underwear, he slides on his jeans and pulls a sweater over his head, dressing for a mercy mission. He asks me how to say *termometro* in English, and because its pronounciation is close to the Italian, he can't differentiate the two. I write it on a Post-it along with "Tylenol and something for flu." It hurts desperately to laugh, but I laugh anyway. Fernando says hysteria is common in cases like this. He checks his money.

He has lire and two gold Krugerrands. I tell him the pharmacy takes only dollars, and he throws up his hands, saying how little time there is to waste. He bundles into his jacket, wraps around his muffler, tugs his furry hat into place, and stretches a glove over his left hand, the right-hand one having disappeared into the ether over the Atlantic. Girded for the wars he might face in the forty-degree sunshine during the three-block journey west into Clayton, the Venetian departs. This is to be his very first solo socioeconomic encounter in America. He comes back into the house to fetch his dictionary, kissing me twice again, shaking his head in disbelief that I could have invited such tragedy.

Full of warm tea and all the little pills and potions with which the Venetian has plied me, I sleep most of the day and into the night. Once, when I awaken, I find him sitting on the edge of the bed facing me, his eyes pools of sweetness. "The fever has passed, you're lovely and cool now. *Dormi, amore mio, dormi*. Sleep, my love, sleep." I look at him, at his narrow hunched shoulders, his face still a picture of worry. He gets up to adjust the blanket, and I look at him bending over me in his sensible knee-length woolen underwear. I think he looks like the skinny man on the beach before he wrote away for his copy of "Muscle Culture." I think he is the most gorgeous thing I've ever seen.

I ask him, "Did you think I was going to die?"

He says, "No. But I was frightened. You were very sick. You still are, and now you must sleep again. But you know, just in case you *do* die before I die, I have a plan, a way to find you. I don't desire to wait another fifty years, and so I'll go to Saint Peter and I'll ask directly for the kitchen, for the wood-burning oven, to be exact. Do you think there's a bread oven in Paradise? If there is, there you'll be, all full of flour and smelling like rosemary." He tells me all this while he pulls at the sheets, attempting knife-edge military corners. Finally content with his adjustments, he sits near to me again and, in a whispery baritone, the Venetian stranger who looks very much like Peter Sellers and a little like Rudolf Valentino sings a lullabye. He caresses my forehead and says, "You know I've always wanted someone to sing to me, but now I know that what I want more is to sing to you."

Next morning, tracking the scent of his burning cigarette, I run out toward the living room. "You should not be get upping," he tells me in English, chasing me back into bed. He climbs in next to me and we sleep. We sleep the sleep of children.

On the morning of the day he is to depart for Venice we forgo our fireside chat, we leave coffee in our cups. We don't stop by the café. We don't even talk very much. We walk a long time through the park and then find a bench on which to rest for a while. A flock of geese are honking and flapping their way exuberantly through cold crystal air. "Aren't they a little late getting south?" I ask him.

"A little," he says. "Perhaps they were waiting for one of them to catch up or, perhaps, they were lost. It's only important that now they are on their way. Like us," he says.

"How poetic you are," I tell him.

"A few weeks ago I would have never even looked up at those birds, I would have never even heard them. Now I feel part of things. Yes, I feel *connected*. I think that's the word. I feel already married to you, as if I've always been married to you but I just couldn't find you. It even seems unnecessary to ask you to marry me. It seems better to say, please don't get lost again. Stay close. Stay very close to me." His is the shadowy voice of a boy saying secrets.

~

After returning home from the airport that evening, I light a fire in the hearth in my bedroom and throw cushions down in front of it as he had done each evening. I sit there where he had sat, pull his woolen undershirt over my nightgown and feel as small and fragile as I can remember. It has all been settled. He is to begin moving papers about in Venice in preparation for our marriage. I am to close up my life in America and get to Italy as quickly as I can, looking to June as the absolute latest date. I decide to sleep by the fire, and I pull a blanket off the bed and lie down under it. I inhale the scent of the stranger, which rises from his shirt. I love this smell. "I love Fernando," I tell myself and the fire. I am bewildered by this fresh new fact of my life, more from the swiftness of its coming than by its truth. I search for some sense of folie à deux. I find none. Rather than being love-blinded, it is in love that I can see, really see.

Never was there even a flickering sense of my having been beckoned up onto a white horse by a curly-haired swain, by the man-who-would-be-king, my one-and-only-meant-to-be-mine. I never felt the earth crack open. Never. What I felt, what I feel, is *quiet.* Except for those first hours together in Venice, there has been no confusion, no confounding, none of the measuring and considering one might think to be natural for a woman up to her knees in middle age who thinks to jump the moat. Now all the doors are open, and there is warm yellow light behind them. This does not feel like a new perspective but like the first and only perspective that has ever belonged only to me, the first perspective that has been neither compromised nor redrawn. Fernando is a first choice. I never had to talk myself into loving him, to balance out his merits and defects on a yellow pad. Nor did I have to, once again, remind myself that I wasn't getting any younger, that I should be grateful for the attentions of yet another "very nice man."

Too often it is we who won't let life be simple. Why must we squeeze it and bite it and slam it against what we've convinced ourselves are our great powers of reason? We violate the innocence of things in the name of rationality so we can wander about, uninterrupted, in our search for passion and sentiment. *Let the inexplicable sit sacred.* I love him. Skinny legs, narrow shoulders, sadness, tenderness, beautiful hands, beautiful voice, wrinkled knees. No saxophone. No airplanes. Jesuit ghosts.

I wait for sleep that doesn't come. It's nearly three in the morning, and I remember that in five and a half hours the real estate broker and her agents will be arriving, en masse, for a look at the house. I wonder about my audience with the Italian consulate in Saint Louis, whom I've heard is a witchy Sicilian. I understand how much I have taken on with the stranger but, more, I know that whatever else might happen, I am in love for the first time in my life.

# 3

# Why Shouldn't I Go to Live on the Fringes of an Adriatic Lagoon with a Blueberry-Eyed Stranger?

*A* stunning cold wakens me. Dull thin snowlight shows itself from behind the window's white lace. White on white, and Fernando is gone. I run to raise the thermostat, then back to the window to watch the spectacle. A foot or so of icy snow has already fallen on the terrace. Would the real estate agents still come? Should I wait to begin polishing up things? I wander through the rooms, which seem bigger or smaller now, empty without his open suitcases and shoes and all his highly colored cargo festooning them. I miss the disorder that went away with him. How unlike me. I remember back to the June morning when I closed on this house. I had played the unflinching martinet, running my hands over surfaces, tsk-tsking over paint splatters on the mahogany satin floors, threatening to halt the proceedings because of a quirky garage door opener. The restructuring of the house had been a yearlong saga, ten months of which were conducted long-distance from Sacramento. "A fireplace in the kitchen, the bedroom, and the living room?" sneered the contractor during our initial meeting. During the final two months of work I had stayed at Sophie's—she being a new friend, a woman in a transition of her own, who sought company at least as much as the income she earned from renting rooms in her musty old house. I would spend hours each day on-site, deep in some little project of my own or sometimes running and fetching for the workers. I thought back to the great painters' rebellion on the morning I began with, "You see, I'd like each room to be painted in an almost imperceptibly descending tint of terra-cotta." I'd spilled a sackful of color chips onto the floor. "And the dining room, I would like it to be in this clear, bright sort of primary red," I continued, brandishing a swatch of damask.

"Red, really red, like your lipstick?" asked one of them incredulously.

"Ah, that's exactly it. Lipstick red," I smiled in perfect satisfaction at his quick comprehension. Besides, what's so odd about red? Red is earth and stone and sunset and barns and schoolhouses, and certainly red can be the walls of a little candlelit room where people sit down together to supper.

"It will take six, maybe eight coats to get an even coverage with a color that dark, ma'am," warned another. "It's gonna make the space feel smaller, closed-in," he said.

"Yes, the space will be warm, inviting," I said as though we were in agreement.

I remembered going to visit the painters during their work, bringing them cold tea and the first fat ripe cherries still warm from Sophie's tree. And when the opus was finished and nearly every one of the workers, all of them spiffed and scented, came to the house-warming, it was the painting squad who photographed the rooms from a hundred angles, two of them coming back again and again to shoot the spaces in changing light. The sweet little house, made with so much love, had, after all, been an obsession, short-lived. All I wished for now was to be free of it, to leave it fast behind me, to go and live in a house I'd never seen, a place Fernando wincingly described as "a very small apartment in a postwar condominium that needs a lot of work."

"What sort of work?" I'd asked brightly. "Paint and furniture? New drapes?"

"More precisely, there are many things to put in order." I waited. He proceeded, "Nothing much has been done since its construction in the early fifties. My father owned it as a rental property. I inherited it from him."

I skewed my imaginings toward the grotesque, hoping to avoid later delusion. I pictured small-windowed square rooms, lots of Milanese plastic, mint green and flamingo pink paint peeling everywhere. Weren't those the colors of postwar Italy? It would have been nice if he'd told me he lived in a third-floor, frescoed flat in a Gothic palazzo that looked over the Grand Canal or, perhaps, in the former atelier of Tintoretto, where the light would be splendid. But he didn't. It wasn't for Fernando's house that I was going to Venice.

I missed him desperately, even sniffed about for some remnant of his cigarette smoke. As I walked through the living room I could see him there, his Peter Sellers grin, arms folded at the elbows inward toward his chest, fingers beckoning me. "Come here to dance with me," he'd say, as his newly acquired, enormously esteemed Roy Orbison disk sobbed through the stereo. I would always lay down my book or my pen, and we would dance. I want to dance now, barefoot, shaking in the cold. How I want to dance with him. I

remember the people waltzing in Piazza San Marco. Was I really
going to live there? Was I really going to marry Fernando?

Terror, illness, deceit, delusion, marriage, divorce, loneliness had
all come to visit early enough in my life, interfering with the peace.
Some of the demons just passed through, while others of them
pitched tents outside my back door. And they stayed. One by one
they went away, each leaving some impression of the visit that made
me stronger, better. I'm thankful the gods were impatient with me,
that they never waited until I was thirty or fifty or seventy-seven,
that they'd had the grace to throw down the gauntlets when I was so
young. Gauntlets are the stuff of every life, but when you learn,
young, how to pick them up, how to work them against the demons,
and, finally, how to outlast if not escape those same demons, life can
seem more merciful. It's that long, smooth, false swanning through
the course of a life that seems to drive a person, sooner or later, into
the wall. I never swanned through anything, but I was always grateful for the chance to keep trying to shine up things. Anyway, by this
time, there wasn't much left to fear. A grim childhood, scattered
here and there with the hideous, provided early grief and shame.
I kept thinking it must be me who was all wrong, me that was so
dreadful, me the cause of the epic agony in my family. No one worked
very hard to dissuade me from my thinking. Why couldn't I live in
a house with golden windows where people were happy, where no
one had bad dreams or white-hot fear? I wanted to be anywhere
where someone wasn't lashing old pain across my new life, flailing it
smart as a leather strap.

When I understood it was me, myself, who'd have to build the
house with the golden windows, I got to work. I salved heartaches,

learned to bake bread, raised children, invented a life that felt good.
And now I'm choosing to leave that life. I let myself remember my
quaking fears when the children were small, the lean periods, my
playing for time with the gods, asking to stay strong and well enough
to take care of them, to grow them up a while longer. Isn't that what
single moms do? We fear someone stronger than us will take away
our babies. We fear someone will find grievous fault with the job
we're doing, with the choices we're making. We're already hard
enough on ourselves. And even in our strengths, we're judged broken. At best, we're half-good. We fear poverty and solitude. *Lady
Madonna, children at her feet.* We fear breast cancer. We fear our children's fear. We fear the speed at which their childhood passes. *Wait.
Wait, please, I think I understand it now. I think I can do it better. Can we
just repeat last month? How did you get to be thirteen? How did you get
to be twenty? Yes. Yes, of course, you must leave. Yes, I understand. I love you,
baby. I love you, Mommy.*

At first, I talked more often than usual to Lisa and Erich, my children. I would call, and they would ask a million questions I wasn't
certain how to answer, or they would call just to hear if I was okay,
if I was having doubts or that sort of thing. After a few weeks we
spoke less frequently and with strain. They needed to talk more to
each other than to me during this time, having to sort out shock and
joy and fear, perhaps. Lisa would call and I would cry and she would
just say, "Mom, I love you."

Erich came to visit. He took me to dinner at Balaban's and sat
across the table searching my face hard. Satisfied, then, that at least I
looked the same, he sat a long time sipping quietly at his wine. At last
he opened with, "I hope you're not frightened about all this. It will

be good for you." It was a vintage tactic of his to reassure me when it was he who was drop-dead scared of something.

"No, I'm not frightened," I said, "and I hope you're not either."

"Frightened? No. I just need to readjust my compass. You and home have always been in the same place," he said.

"And they still are. It's just that now home and I will be in Venice," I told him.

I knew the difference between going off to university, knowing that home is a few hundred miles away, and having one's mother dissolve that home to go and live in Europe. Now home would be six thousand miles away, not accessible on long weekends. And there was also this person called Fernando. It was altogether a less dramatic event for my daughter, she having lived in Boston for several years already, deep in romance, her studies, her work. I wished my children could feel part of this future of mine, but all this wasn't happening to the three of us together, as most events that had happened before in our lives. This time something was happening only to me. A part of me knew we were an old team, inseparable by a sea. Another part knew that their childhood was ending and that, in a strange way, my childhood was beginning.

The really precious parts of my life are transportable, not conditions of geography. Why shouldn't I go to live on the fringes of an Adriatic lagoon with a blueberry-eyed stranger and leave no trail of biscotti crumbs to find my way back? My house, my fancy car, even my native country were not, by definition, me. My sanctuary, my sentimental self were veteran travelers. And they would go where I would.

⌐

I shake off the reverie and put on the kettle, start my bath, call the café to see if the baker has arrived on time and sober and set Paganini at a gentle volume. The real estate agents will soon be here.

Rather than racing about to clean the whole house, I opt for the more elemental seduction of crackling fires and the scent of some cinnamon-dusted thing wafting from the oven. Once I have flames leaping in all three hearths, I cut up some three-day-old scone dough left from one of Fernando's breakfasts, top the little pillows with spice and sugar and great dollops of butter and close the oven door as the bell rings. I greet the throng, which arrives together, despite the storm, as though on divine command. The brigade files past me, tossing coats and scarves onto a divan, revealing their smart mustardy blazers, and, without ceremony, commences inspection. There are eleven agents in all. The restrained murmurs of approval soon give way to delighted screams as one opens the door into the pewter-papered guest bath, another looks up at the nineteenth-century Austrian crystal dripping from the living-room ceiling and yet another eases herself down into the coppery velvet plumpness of the wingback chair in front of the kitchen fire.

"Who was your architect?"

"Who did the work on this place?"

"Your decorator must be from Chicago."

"My God, this is fabulous," says the only gentleman among the women. "Why on earth do you want to sell this?"

"I know," stage-whispers someone else. "It's so romantic it makes me feel frumpy."

"You *are* frumpy," the gentleman assures her.

"How can you bear to part with it?" asks another.

It was clearly my turn to speak. "Well, I'm leaving it because I'm going to marry a Venetian." Big breath. "I'm going to live in Venice," I say gently, deliciously, trying out the words. Was that me, was that my voice? The brigade responds with a long silence. When one begins to speak, all of them do.

"How old are you?"

"How did you meet this man?"

"Is he a count or something?" asks one, eager to embroider the text.

Mostly, I think, they want to know if he is rich. To say outright that he is relatively poor would perplex them, nick away at their fantasy, so I opt for a part of the truth. "No, he's not a count. He's a banker who looks just like Peter Sellers," I say.

"Oh, honey. Be careful." It's the frumpy one speaking. "Have him checked out, I mean, really checked out. Four years ago my friend Isabelle met up with a Neapolitan on Capri, and he almost bamboozled her into a quick marriage until one night she woke up and heard him mooning, whispering into his cell phone from the terrace outside their hotel room. He'd had the nerve to tell her he'd only been saying good-night to his mother."

Her story seems some inappropriate cocktail of low-level envy and a genuine desire to protect me. She doesn't know Fernando, I think. That I don't know him either seems irrelevant.

One of them, trying to rescue the more symphonic motif of the tale comes in with, "I'll bet he has a gorgeous house. What's it like?"

"Oh, I don't think there's much that's gorgeous about it. He lives in a 1950s condominium on the beach. Actually, I haven't seen it yet," I say.

"You mean you're selling your home and cashing in your whole life without. . . ." Her query is overruled by the gentleman who aims to comfort the crowd.

"Maybe it's Venice you're in love with. If I had a chance to move to Venice, I wouldn't give two hoots for what the house was like." They sally and banter without me.

When the brigade exits, one agent stays behind to write an offer to buy my house herself. The offer is serious, reasonable, not so many thousands of dollars less than the price Fernando and I had talked about with my attorney. She tells me she has long been planning to end her marriage, leave her job, and start an agency of her own. She says that finding this house with the lipstick-red dining room is the last button necessary to activate her renaissance program.

"I won't be leaving behind any magic dust here," I warn. "If you buy this house it doesn't mean you'll fall in love with a charming Spaniard or something like that. It's just a pretty little, regular house," I say inanely, wanting to protect her from her impulse and, perhaps, me from mine. "Why don't you think about it and we can talk later," I continue without looking at her and as though I was big and she was little.

"How long did you think about it before you said yes to your Venetian? This is all happening just as it should," she says with a voice that came from a misty place inside her. "I'd like you to tell me what furniture you are willing to sell," she continues. I learned much later that, with some deft caressing of the zoning laws, my red dining room became the office from which she operates her independent agency.

⌐

I call my children. I call my attorney. Fernando calls me. I call Fernando. Was it all going to be this simple? I pull off my good black dress and pull on jeans and boots, remembering I had to place an order with the meat purveyor before ten. I ring up Mr. Wasserman without thinking first what I'd cook for that evening's menu. I hear myself telling him I'll need baby lamb shanks, fifty of them. I'd never yet cooked baby lamb shanks at the café. Used to my orders for game and veal, Mr. Wasserman misses half a beat, then assures me they"ll be delivered before three. "How will you cook them?" he wants to know.

"I'll braise them in a saffron tomato broth, lay them over French lentils and add a stripe of black olive paste," my chef's voice announces without consulting me.

"Write me in for two at seven-thirty, will you?" he says. After a look at the ice-encrusted car, I walk the mile or so to the café, though I'd never once walked to work before. Of course I'd never been romantic about old smoke from an Italian cigarette left behind in my bedroom, either. And those baby lamb shanks. Tramping through high snow that is falling still in earnest, my old white Mother Russia coat trailing, making a soft, scraping noise behind me. I wonder when I will begin, if I will begin at all, to feel sad about all these endings I was sealing. Would there be some late lapse of courage? Is it, indeed, courage that was shaping my way? Is it

bravado? Did I fancy myself some aging armchair swashbuckler setting off, at last, to adventure? No. My friend Misha says I am *la grande
cocotte* with flour on my hands. Or ink stains. No, I'd never been an
"armchair" anything. And let's go back to why I must anticipate anguish or muddy what was feeling immensely clear. There is nothing
I want more than to be with Fernando. Anyway, June seems far off,
safely, sadly far away.

As I near the corner of Pershing and DeBalivier I remember there
is to be a meeting with my partners before lunch. A father and son,
the elder is a rancorous old magistrate, the younger, a gentle-
hearted philosopher who is restaurateuring to please his magiste-
rial old papa. That it is papa's choice to never be pleased has yet to
impress the son. It's a brief, cool discourse between us, an almost
luscious divorce, and we agree that June 15, the day after our last
programmed event and one year, to the day, from when I'd moved
into my house, would be my last. I call Fernando. He says to book
my ticket even though it is only December 19. It is not yet noon,
and I've sold my house and drawn up a graceful exit from a piece of
my business. All that's left to do now is the slow braising of fifty baby
lamb shanks.

# 4

# Did It Ever Happen to You?

Before Fernando returned to Venice, we had scribbled a
time line of sorts, establishing priorities and settling on
definitive dates by which everything would be accomplished. It was he who thought it best to sell the house immediately
rather than rent it for a while, to wait and see. Sell the car, too, he
had said. And the few pieces of good artwork, the furnishings. I
should come to Italy with only those things that were absolutely *in-
dispensabili.* I balked until I remembered the talk I'd already had with
myself about "house, fancy car, etc." Still, I thought him callous,
talking as he did about the house as though it were only a pretty
container in which I would wait until it was time to go, a nicely
decorated launchpad. But, also, I remembered another talk I'd had
with myself after knowing Fernando only a few days. He needed to
lead.

I already knew how to lead. For better and for worse, I had always been more than ready to carve away at life whenever the fates
left me a little room. But he had been a sleepy observer of his life,
watching its events and embracing them in a kind of passive obedi-
ence. He said that telephoning me that afternoon when we first saw
each other in Venice and, more, chasing me back to America were

among the first acts of sheer will he'd ever dared to undertake. Fragile, I think. There is a new gossamer-thin self-awareness about him, and Fernando needs desperately to be in charge. So be it. As much as I know how to lead I know how to follow, when I trust someone. But I know, too, that the following sometimes chafes.

"Let's just begin at the beginning," said he who'd lived his most of his life in two apartments on an island less than a mile wide and seven miles long, said he who'd gone to work in a bank at age twenty-three when what he really wanted was to fly airplanes and play the saxophone. Yet, unsolicited, his father had secured a post for him and then laid out a new suit and shirt and tie on his bed, new shoes on the floor below it, and told Fernando they'd be waiting for him at the bank at eight the next morning. He went. And he goes there still. It was curious, his telling me to be a beginner when so many things in his life would remain exactly as they were. Or would they?

And so I had to decide what would go over the sea and what would stay, and the most puzzling things made the short list. A small oval table, black, marble-topped with ornate carved legs; nearly a hundred crystal wineglasses (going to the kingdom of hand-blown glass!); too many books, too few photos, fewer clothes than I thought I would take (the waitresses in the café were presented with a life's worth of Loehmann's and Syms's final markdowns); an old Ralph Lauren quilt; a set of antique sterling flatware (packed and shipped separately for reasons of security and which never arrived in Venice); and pillows, dozens of small, less small, tasseled, corded, ruffled, chintz, silk, tapestry, velvet pillows, like so many pieces of so many places where I'd lived. Small evidences of past lives, I thought. Proof of my well-decorated nests. Were they, perhaps, to cushion my landing?

Much of the rest, I divvied up into small legacies. Sophie was transforming a spare bedroom into an office; hence, she got the French desk. I knew my friend Luly wanted the baker's rack, and so we stuffed it into the backseat of her car one evening. There were many such scenes. And rather than being sad at parting with so much, I found my new and relative minimalism exhilarating. I felt as though I'd weeded, scrubbed, dug in the earth clear down to China.

❧

My waiting days were full. The café in the morning, writing in the afternoon, back to the café for final prep. I fitted in meetings, way out on the godforsaken edges of the city, with the Italian consulate, which comprised a battered old wooden desk, an older Smith Corona portable, and an older yet *palermitana*—a woman from Palermo—the wife of the insurance agent in whose office the consulate was situated. *La signora* was aubergine-haired, thick at her middle, and had spindly legs. Her fingernails were painted bright red, and she sucked at cigarettes in a hungry, hollow-cheeked way. She somehow pulled the smoke up into her nose and into her mouth at the same time, then tilted her head back and sent the last wisps of it curling upward, all the while holding the smoldering thing between those red-tipped fingers and up close to her cheek. She whispered a lot. It was as though her husband—two yards away and seated at a huge formica desk—shouldn't be privy to our discourse.

She pecked away on the Smith Corona, preserving my life's story on sheaves of official paper provided by the Italian government.

My personal data, my motive for moving to Italy, testimonies of my free and unmarried state and my upright citizenship, the size of the bankroll with which I would enter my new country, premarital documents to satisfy the state, premarital documents to satisfy the church—all were transcribed. It was a work that might have been accomplished in less than forty efficient minutes, but the lady from Palermo saw fit to extend the task over four full-morning congresses. The signora wanted to talk. She wanted to be sure, she whispered through her smoke, I knew what I was doing. "What do you know about Italian men?" she challenged, from under her dark-shadowed, half-closed eyes. I only smiled. Miffed at my silence, she typed faster and stamped the papers viciously, repeatedly, with the great inked seal of the Italian state. She tried again. "They're all *mammoni,* mama's boys. That's why I married an American. Americans are less *furbi,* less cunning," she whispered. "All they want is a big-screen television, to play golf on Saturday, go off to Rotary Club on Wednesday, and to watch, once in a while, when you're dressing. They never complain about food as long as it's meat and it's hot and it's served before six o'clock. Have you ever cooked for an Italian man?," she whispered more loudly.

As her inquiries became more intimate, she typed and stamped more furiously. She told me to leave my money in an American bank, to put my furniture in storage. I'd be back within a year, she said. She saved for last her story of the Illinois blonde who divorced her handsome politician husband to marry a Roman who already had a wife whom he kept in Salerno and, as it turned out, a Dutch boyfriend to whom he made monthly visits in Amsterdam. I paid her arbitrary and exaggerated fees, took my thick, perfectly executed portfolio, accepted her airy Marlboro-scented kisses, and drove away, wondering about this compulsion some women seemed to have about saving me from the stranger.

The evenings I spent almost always alone, in a soft sort of idleness. Before leaving the café, I'd pack up some small choice thing for my supper and be home by eight. I'd pull Fernando's same old woolen undershirt, still unwashed, over my nightgown, light a fire in one room or another, and pour a glass of wine. Looking for that same good sensation of having *weeded, scrubbed, and dug clear down to China,* which I'd earned from sorting through my material cache, now I wanted to look at things more spiritual than silver teapots and armoires. I wanted to be ready for this marriage.

I challenged ghosts, looking backward into long-ago shadows lit with old, strangely palpable tableaux. I could see my grandmother's sweet, teary eyes and the two of us kneeling by her bed to say the rosary. I always finished before she finished because I skipped every third bead. She knew, but she never scolded me. I learned about mystery from her. Or maybe it was that mystery was as natural and easy for both of us as it was to weep or weed the scrawny patch of hollyhocks and zinnias against the shed out back. It was easy to walk down to Rosy's or to the coffee lady's, up the three steep steps and into Perreca's for two loaves of bread—one round crunchy loaf for supper, one round crunchy loaf for the block-and-a-half walk back home. She was contained, closed even, to most others, but together my grandmother and I would tell secrets. When I was still too young to really understand, she told me about her little boy.

He was five, I think, or perhaps younger, and each morning she would awaken him before the rest of the family, sending him to race across the narrow street in front of the house to the railroad tracks to gather coal for the old iron stove. Together, then, they would make a fire, set the coffee brewing and the bread toasting, before they tugged everyone else awake. One morning, as she stood at the kitchen window, watching him as she always did, a short line of B&O freight wagons came careening around the curve, way off schedule. Out of nowhere. Her screaming choked by hurtling steel, she watched the train crush her baby. Walking alone to where he lay, wrapping him in her skirts, she carried him home.

When my babies were born and, maybe even before that, I began to understand why she'd freely told me the story that she'd never been able to recount to anyone in the then half century since its happening. Of course, people knew the story, but no one had ever heard it from her. She'd lived through the most horrific of human injuries, and her telling of it was a legacy: it gave me a perspective that would serve me always, a prism through which I would examine my own injuries, to give their weight and their solution a just energy.

I had far too few days to spend with my grandmother. I used to wish I was older than all her children, older than she was, so I could take care of her. But she died alone in the early twilight of a December afternoon. Snow fell. And the rags of my illusion about family died with her. The pain of childhood loneliness still haunts me. But life was round, sweet during those flitting moments when my grandmother was holding my hand, whenever she was close enough for me to catch the scent of her. It is still.

In those solitary evenings by my fire I found finely spun threads, a pattern, my own story. I opened up the kind of memory that feels like a wistful hankering for something lost or something that never was. I think most of us have it, this potentially destructive habit of mental record-keeping that builds, distorts, then breaks up and spreads into even the farthest flung territories of reason and consciousness. What we do is accumulate the pain, collect it like cranberry glass. We display it, stack it up into a pile. Then we stack it up into a mountain so we can climb up onto it, waiting for, demanding sympathy, salvation. "Hey, do you see this? Do you see how big my pain is?" We look across at other people's piles and measure them, shouting, "My pain is bigger than your pain." It's all somehow like the medieval penchant for tower building. Each family demonstrated its power with the height of its own personal tower. One more layer of stone, one more layer of pain, each one a measure of power.

I'd always fought to keep dismantling my pile, to sort and reject as much of the clutter as I could. Now, even more, I made myself look back straight into that which was over and done with, and that which would never be. I was determined to go to Fernando, and if there was to be some chance for us to take our story beyond this beginning, I knew I would have to go lightly. I was fairly certain the stranger's piles would provide enough work for both of us.

⌒

Except with my children, I had little conversation with anyone during those last months in Saint Louis. It was my own counsel I wanted to keep. There were two exceptions. Misha, my friend from Los Angeles, came to visit, condemning my intentions to marry

Fernando, placing them neatly into the ranks of midlife crisis. Milena saw things differently. My best friend, a Florentine who had been living in California for more than thirty of her then fifty-six years, Milena was characterisically severe and talked mostly with her eyes. Trying to read her by telephone was maddening. I would have to face her if I wanted to know what she was thinking about my news. I went to Sacramento to visit, and only then, sitting in front of those sharp, dark eyes, could I feel her acceptance. "Take it in both your hands and hold tight to this love. If it comes, it comes only once."

When I told her about Misha's cynical predictions, Milena called him a two-penny prophet whose oracles might even be true. And, with eyes looking far away, chin tilted up, mouth pursed, she banished Misha's gloom with a wave of her beautiful brown hand. "If this is love, if there is even the possibility that this is real love, what do you care? What will it cost you to live it out? Too much? Everything? Now that it has presented itself to you, could you dare to imagine turning away from it for anything or anyone?" She lit a cigarette and pulled at it fiercely. She had already finished talking.

"Did it ever happen to you?" I asked. Her cigarette was nearly a stub by the time she answered.

"Yes, I think it did happen once to me. But I was afraid the sentiments would change. I was afraid of some form of betrayal and so I walked away. I betrayed *it* before it could betray me. And maybe I thought life inside that intensity would suffocate me. So I chose a sort of pleasant, safe compromise, an emotion less than passion and more than tolerance. Isn't that what most of us choose?" she asked.

"I find the *intensity* beautiful. I've never felt more serene than since I met Fernando," I told her. She laughed.

"You would be serene in hell. You'd start cooking and baking and redecorating. You are your own serenity. It didn't come from nor can it go away because of Fernando," she said. Milena's cancer was diagnosed that next fall. She died on the night of Christmas, 1998.

❧

Too quickly, too slowly, June arrives, and on the night before departure, Erich comes to stay with me. The house is as empty as a barn. On my bedroom floor we make two pallets of the packing quilts left behind by the movers, cover them with fresh sheets borrowed from Sophie, finish the last of the Grand Marnier, and talk away the night, liking the echoes that our voices make in the empty house. Next morning we say good-bye easily enough, having settled that he will come to Venice for the month of August. The shuttle driver, Erich, and two neighbors heave my baggage into the van. My new minimalism seems to have gained weight.

It takes half an hour to wheel and drag everything into the terminal and over to Alitalia. The overweight fees are too terrible to pay, and I wish I had heeded Fernando's good advice about bringing only what is *indispensabile*. There is nothing to do but unpack and stage an auction right here in front of check-in.

The ticket agents unzip and unbuckle while I pull out treasures. I inaugurate the event. "Would anyone like this Limoges chocolate set?" Then, "Here's a suitcaseful of hats, winter hats, straw hats, veils, feathers, flowers. Anyone for hats?" Soon there is a gathering of travelers and passersby, some just gaping, some happily, incredulously taking things off my hands. I am offering up a case of '85 Chateau Montelena cabernet and a trunkful of shoes when the captain of my flight saunters by with his equipage. We recognize each other from different lives: his as an occasional guest at the café, mine as "that lady chef." He stops. I offer an abridged recitation of my story and, after a short conference with an agent, he motions me to follow him, bending down to whisper, "Everything will be taken care of."

A steward ushers me into the first-class waiting room, another sets down a tray with a bottle of Schramsberg Blanc de Noir and a flute. One pops the cork, pours, hands me the glass by its stem. I'm impressed. At twenty-second intervals I sip, fiddle with my shiny new Casedei sandals, take my hair down, and tie it back up again. I keep trying to remember to breathe. A woman of, perhaps, fifty, wearing a Stetson, alligator boots, and capri pants sits down next to me, avoiding the other six tenantless leather couches.

"Are you a woman in transformation?" she begins. I'm not sure I've heard her correctly and so I just continue to spit-polish my shoes while flashing her a smile of welcome.

She asks me again, and this time I have no choice but to believe my ears and so I answer her, "Well, I think we all are. I hope we all are. I mean, isn't life, itself, transformation?" She looks at me with craven pity, tilting her head, preparing to illuminate my innocence, when I am rescued by an attendant and escorted up into the penthouse of the 747, far away from my original coach position.

I am fed and coddled by the staff and given much attention from the four Milanese businessmen who are my cabin companions. After everyone is settled down, chocolates and cognac duly consumed, the captain opens his microphone with wishes for all our sweet dreams. He adds that, in honor of the American woman who is going to Venice to be married, he will take the liberty of singing an old Roberto Carlos song. At thirty thousand feet, all husky and sensual, he croons. *"Veloce come il vento voglio correre da te, per venire da te, per vivere con te.* Fast as the wind I want to run to you, to come to you, to live with you."

At sunrise I am still awake. The little cabin is washed in new June light, and I pretend to breakfast as though it is any normal morning. The balladeer masquerading as our captain announces our descent over Milan. I sit there in tremors, emotions tumbling, colliding, an icy free fall from one life into the next. I clutch the seat arms as though they and the quick hard beating of my heart could force the great hulking machine down faster or make it stay still. A last attempt at control, perhaps. I'd descended upon Italy so many times before, a traveler, a visitor with a return ticket. I have time only to wipe my face dry, to take my hair down and put it up one more time. We touch ground with the gentlest *thump.*

# 5

# Savonarola Could Have Lived Here

*T* *hump.* The first carriageful of suitcases is thrust through the swinging doors from the baggage claim out into the horrid yellow and black of Malpensa airport. The good captain had seen to it that all my things, except those already given away, arrived with me. *Thump.* A frontier guard, shepherding things, leaves his automatic weapon dangling from his belt as he forces one cart after another out into the arrival area while I look on. *"Buona permanenza, signora,"* says the guard sotto voce and barely moving his mouth. "A happy stay for you, my lady. I hope he is a true gentleman."

"How do you know that a man is waiting for me?" I ask him.

*"C'è sempre un uomo,"* he answers with a salute. "There's always a man." I sling two carry-ons over squared shoulders and follow my bags out into the crowd of those waiting. I hear him before I see him.

*"Ma, tu sei tutta nuda,"* he is saying from behind a sheaf of yellow daisies, yellow, like the Izod shirt he wears loose over green plaid slacks. He looks like a technicolor anchovy, so thin—small almost —standing among the others behind the cordons. Blueberry eyes set in sun-bronzed skin, so different from his winter face. I am going to marry that stranger there in the yellow Izod shirt, I say to myself. I am going to marry a man whom I've never known in sum-

mer. This is the first time I've walked toward him while he stood still. Everything around him in sepia, only Fernando is in color. Even now whenever I come upon him, meet him in a restaurant, under the clock tower at noon, at the potato lady's table in the market, in our own dining room when it's full of friends, I flash back to that scene and, for half a moment, once again only he is in color.

"But you're all naked," he is saying again, crushing me into the daisies he still holds tight to his chest with one hand. My legs are bare, stretching up from my new sandals to a short navy skirt and a white T-shirt. He's never seen me in summer either. We stay fixed, quiet for a long time in that first embrace. We are shy. We are comfortably shy.

Most of the bags and cases we fit into the the car's trunk and backseat, neat as fish in a tin. What's left he secures to the roof with a length of plastic rope. *"Pronta?"* he asks. "Ready?" A blithe trans-figuration of Bonnie and Clyde off to burgle the romance of our lives, we race northwest at eighty miles per hour. The air condi-tioner is blasting out great puffs of icy air, the windows are rolled down, inviting in the already hot, wet air outside. He must have both.

Elvis purls out his heart. Fernando knows all the words but only phonetically. "What does it mean?" he wants to know. "I can't stop loving you. It's useless to try." I translate lyrics that I'd never before paid attention to, words he'd been listening to forever. "I've missed you since I was fourteen," he says. "At least that's when I began to notice that I missed you. Maybe it was even earlier. Why did you wait so long to come to me?" There is about all this a sensation of mise-en-scène. I wonder if he feels it. Could anything really be this good? I, who think Shostakovich a modernist, belt out "I can't stop loving you" into the great plain of the Padana stretched out flat and treeless over Italy's unlovely industrial belly. Perhaps this is the date I was always expecting to have.

Two and a half hours later, we take the exit for Mestre, the belching, black-breathed port that warehouses petroleum for all of north Italy. Can it be true that Venice lives cheek to cheek with this horror? Almost immediately there is the bridge, the Ponte della Libertà, the Bridge of Liberty, five miles of it, raised up a scant fifteen feet and hurled out over the waters, riveting Venice to terra firma, dry land. We're nearly home. It's high noon under a straight-up sun, and the lagoon is a great smashed mirror that glints and blinds. We eat thick trenchers of crusty bread laid with ruffles of mortadella, lunch from the little bar in the car park while we wait for the ferry that will carry us to the Lido.

It is a forty-minute cruise on the *Marco Polo,* traversing the lagoon and slicing down the Guidecca Canal to the island that is called Lido di Venezia, the beach of Venice. Thirteen hundred years ago fishermen and farmers lived here. I know that now it is a faded fin de siècle watering hole where, during its heyday, European and American literati came to rest and play. I know that its village of Malamocco, once the Roman settlement of Metamaucus, was the eighth-century seat of the Venetian republic, that the Lido is the stage for the Venice Film Festival, and that there is a casino. And Fernando has told me about it so often, I can imagine the tiny church there, and, in my mind, I can see its plain red stone face looking out to the lagoon. I know that Fernando has lived on the Lido for nearly his whole life. More than this, I have yet to learn.

After the boatman guides the car onto the ferry, Fernando kisses me, looks at me a long time, then says he is going up on deck to smoke. His not inviting me to come along perplexes me, but vaguely. If I really wanted to go upstairs, I would go. I lean back then and close my eyes, trying to remember what I knew I must be forgetting. Was there no work waiting? Nothing left undone? No. Nothing. I have nothing to do, or perhaps is it that I have everything to do? The car leans into the swells of the sea. Maybe it's only me keen to feel some sort of _rhythm_. There is nothing else at this moment but a crisp, fresh, just unrolled space to color. I feel a not unpleasant but curious sort of shift in equilibrium. I _feel_ it. One foot is still six thousand miles away. Just as the boat bumps itself into the jetty, Fernando returns to the car, and we drive off the boat.

In a breezy drive about the island he points out landmarks, personal and cultural. I try to remember how long it's been since I really slept and I compute fifty-one hours. "Please can we go home now?" I ask from my trance. He turns off the Gran Viale Santa Maria Elisabetta, the broad avenue that follows along the seaside of the island, onto a quiet street behind the Film Festival theaters and the very worn chic of the Casino, and then into a narrow _vicolo,_ alleyway, framed in old plane trees whose leaves reach across to each other in a cooling arcade. A great iron gate opens onto a drab courtyard lined in skinny, one-Italian-car garages. Above them rise three levels of windows, most all of which are sheathed in _persiane,_ corrugated metal privacy curtains. Exactly as he promised it, home is inside a postwar concrete bunker. There is no one there except a very small woman of indeterminate age who darts about the car in a kind of tarantella.

"*Ecco Leda.* Here is Leda, our sympathetic gatekeeper," he says. "*Pazza completa.* Completely crazy." She is gazing upward, beseeching. Is she emotional because of our arrival? In fact she offers no greeting, neither uttered, shrugged, nor nodded. "*Ciao,* Leda," he says, without looking at her or introducing us. Leda gargles out something about not leaving the car in front of the entryway too long.

I try, "*Buona sera, Leda. Io sono Marlena.* Good evening, Leda. I'm Marlena."

"*Sei americana?*" she asks. "Are you American?"

"*Si, sono americana,*" I tell her.

"*Mi sembra più francese.* You seem more French to me," she says, as if she means Martian. We unload, she continues the tarantella. Much as I try, I can't resist furtive peeks at her. She is a Faustian troll with black-olive eyes hooded like a hawk's. Over the next three years I will never once hear her laugh, though I will hear her grizzly shrieks and see her fists extended to the heavens more times than I wish to remember. I will learn too that she wears teeth only to mass. But here, now, I romanticize her. All she needs is some tenderness and a warm bitter-chocolate tart, I think.

As we shove and pull my bags along the corridor to the elevator, a few people are in arrival or departure. *Buon giorno. Buona sera.* The dialogue is stingy. We might be hauling cadavers in burlap bags for all they care. On the last trips out to the car, I notice more than one person cantilevered out of as many just-unsheathed windows. *L'americana è arrivata.* The American has arrived. Holding out for a scene from *Cinema Paradiso,* I wait for at least one black-stockinged, kerchiefed old woman to come forth and press me to a generous bosom scented in rosewater and sage. But there is no one.

Elevators are announcements, and, as much as do entry halls, they tell the house's story. This one, its atmospheric composition oxygen-free after fifty years of carting smoking human cargo, is three feet square, paved in linoleum, and painted a shiny aquamarine. Its cables screech and creek under the weight of more than one of us. I read that it is approved to transport three hundred kilos. We send the bags up alone, a few at a time, while we race up three flights to meet them at the apartment door. We do this six times. Fernando can no longer avoid opening the door. He braves it with, *"Ecco la casuccia.* Behold the little house."

At first I can't see a thing except the outlines of cartons and cardboard boxes, which seem to be stacked everywhere. Universal Flood aromas lie thick in the air. With the flicking on of an overhead bulb Fernando illuminates the space, and then I know it's a gag. I hope it's a gag. He has taken me to an abandoned space, some third-floor storage room just for laughs, and so that's what I begin to do. I just laugh and giggle, *"Che bellezza.* How lovely," cupping my face in my hands and shaking my head. Perhaps this is where the black-stockinged old lady comes forth to press me to her bosom and lead me to my real house. I recognize my handwriting on one of the boxes, and it becomes clear that *this* is my real house. Scoured of all vanities, it is the lair of an ascetic, the mean hut of an acolyte. Savonarola could have lived here, all of it bespeaking reverence for a medieval patina, undisturbed by the passing of time or someone's rifling about with a dust cloth. I have come to live in the shuttered-up gloom of Bleak House. I begin to understand the real meaning of Venetian blinds.

The space is astonishingly small, and I think immediately that this is good, that a tiny bleak house will be easier to reform than a large one. Fernando hugs me from behind. I go about lifting the wretched *persiane,* letting in air and sunlight. The kitchen is a cell with a Playskool stove. In the bedroom there is a bizzare oriental carpet covering one wall, a collection of very old ski medals hang from rusty claw-shaped hooks and, like ashen specters, tatters of curtains float over a windowed door that opens to a cramped terrace piled in paint cans. The bed is a double mattress on the floor, a massive and ornate burled-wood headboard leans against the wall behind it. There is perilous walking in the bathroom, what with missing and broken tiles and the great girth of an ancient washing machine dead center between the sink and the bidet. I notice the washer's hose empties out into the bathtub. There are three other tiny rooms whose stories are too terrible to tell. There is no evidence of preparation for his bride's arrival, and he is neither fey nor apologetic when he tells me, "A little at a time, we will make things suit us."

Over and over again he had talked with candor about where and how he lived, that the *where* and *how* were passive symptoms of his life, that the apartment was the space in which he slept, watched television, took a shower. If I am reeling from first-sight shock, it's the fault of my own glossing over. This is neither more nor less than an honest homecoming. It's good that Fernando knows it is for him I have come to Italy, not for his house. Houses are easier to find than are sweet strangers, I think. I think again, this time to a man I knew in California. Jeffrey was an obstetrician, successful, madly in love with Sarah, an artist, starving, who was madly in love with him. After years of fencing, he set Sarah aside for an ophthalmologist, extremely successful, whom he married almost immediately. His rationale was unembarrassed by sentiment. With the doctor, he said, he would have a better house. That is, Jeffrey married a house. This thought soothes me. All this aside, I miss my French canopied bed. I want to drink a good wine out of a beautiful glass. I want a candle and a bath. I want to sleep. As we set about clearing a space on the bed, he says once again what he'd said way back in Saint Louis. "You see, there are *un pò di cosette da fare qui,* a few little things to do here."

~

A sickle moon shows in through the tiny, high-set window in the bedroom. I focus on it, trying to quiet myself for sleep. I'm still on the airplane or maybe in the car, on the ferryboat. I have moved through each leg of the day's odyssey at descending speeds. It's as though, at some point during the journey from there to here, a lapse of sorts has occurred, a short death, during which one era passed the keys onto the next. Rather than being delivered to the *edges* of a new life, I am already inside it, through the looking glass and center stage. Sensations are untethered. I can't sleep. How could I sleep? Now it's me lying here in the Venetian's bed. Fernando sleeps. His breath is warm, constant on my face. Searching for rhythms? Here is a rhythm I think. Very softly I begin to sing. "I can't stop loving you." A lullabye. If it's so that dreams dreamed just before waking are true, what are dreams dreamed just before sleeping? I fall into half-dreams. Half-true?

# 6

# If I Could Give Venice to You for a Single Hour, It Would Be This Hour

*T*he scents of coffee and a newly shaven stranger awaken me. He is standing over the bed with a tray on which sit a tiny battered coffeepot, steaming, and cups, spoons, and sugar in a sack. The house terrifies me in the morning light, but he is luminous. We decide to work for two hours, that whatever order we can wrest from the rubble by then will be enough for the first day. By eleven we are racing down the stairs. He wants to ride out to Torcello, where we can talk and rest and be alone, he says. "Why Torcello?" I ask.

"*Non lo so esattamente.* I don't know exactly. Perhaps because that crumble of earth is even older than Venice." He wants us to begin at the beginning. "Today's my birthday, our birthday, isn't it?" he wants to know.

We settle ourselves on the prow of the vaporetto facing into the wind. It's neither possible nor necessary to speak out there; we squeeze hands. He kisses my eyelids, and, with flapping seagulls for escort, we glide under a Tiepolo sky through abiding lagoons, past abandoned thimblesful of sand, islets that once were market gardens and sheepfolds. We lurch up against the dock at Canale Borgognoni.

Torcello is the ancient mother of Venice, in her lonely yellow leaf. Primitive echoes drift. Here there is a whispering up of secrets: *Take my hand and grow young with me; don't rush, don't sleep; be a beginner; light the candles; keep the fire; dare to love someone; tell yourself the truth; stay inside the rapture.*

It is past two and, with roaring appetite, we take a table under the trees at Ponte del Diavolo, the Devil's Bridge, to eat wood-roasted lamb, arugula dressed with the lamb's own charry juices, and heft after heft of good bread. We eat soft mountain cheeses scribbled with chestnut honey. We sit for a long time until only we are there to keep company with the old waiter—the same one who I remember had served me *risotto coi bruscandoli,* risotto with hop shoots, when I first came to Torcello years before. He still wears a salmon-colored silk cravat and a middle part in his pomaded hair. I like this. Amid so many changes, I feel sympathy in these unbroken facts. Beatifically, the waiter folds napkins as we, also beatifically, dawdle over black cherries, plucked one by one, from a bowl of icy water.

Raised up upon direct order from God to the bishop of Altinum Torcello's Basilica di Santa Maria Assunta is a bedizened shrine to a Byzantine king. Inside its great cavern, the air feels charged, haunted, holy. A great elongated and shadowy Virgin of Byzantium holding Christ looks out, pitiless, from the conch of the apse. A country church with no parish. I ask a monk in brown robes about the hours when mass is said. He brushes past me and floats beyond a tapestry-draped door, my Italian too rustic to earn his response, perhaps. Outside, I run my hand across the marble throne smoothed by a million hands before mine, since the time when Attila sat there, orchestrating doom among the wind-whipped weeds. I want to sleep

out there in that meadow, to rest in its prickly grasses and memories. I want to sleep where the first Venetians slept, sixth-century
fugitive fishermen and shepherds in search of peace and freedom.
From here, the apartment and its medieval patina seem a small
business.

To return to the Lido to rest and change seems a waste of time,
we say, and so we debark from the boat at San Marco. Since I have
packed my purse like an overnight bag, the ladies' room at the
Monaco will be my dressing room. More than once have its aqua
and peachy chintz comforts provided me succor. As I sit before the
mirror, I somehow think of New York, of 488 Madison Avenue
and Herman Associates, how I trundled into the city from upstate
four days each week to write ad copy and "learn the business."
The Hermans would love that I've come across the sea to marry
the stranger. They would take credit for having long ago stirred my
sense of adventure. After all, it was they who sent me off to present
an ad campaign to the government of Haiti just weeks after Baby
Doc fled.

I remember the two men wearing greasy jeans and wide smiles
who accompanied me across an airstrip to a graffitied van and drove,
wordless and pell-mell, through what were the most sorrowful
scenes of human desperation and the most heart-stopping vistas of
natural beauty I have ever seen. Later that first evening, I lay in my
hotel bed under a canopy of patched mosquito netting, breathing in
the thick, sweet air, listening to the drums. Just as in the movies.
Except where is that man from Interpol, the one with the silver hair
and a white dinner jacket, who should be slipping into my room just
about now, enlisting me as accomplice in a night's treachery?

I saw no other American or European woman the week I was in Haiti, the other New York agencies having dispatched fresh-faced boys upholstered in dark blue. An officer of the police force was also a member of the tourism committee. Kind enough to rest his automatic weapon on the table, he sat next to me. My hand brushed the leather strap of it each time I picked up a piece of paper. I began my pitch nervously but gained strength, momentum even, and returned to New York with the account.

Sitting here now, in front of this mirror, I remember racing from the Madison Avenue office most evenings after work to sit for a few moments in front of another mirror, one in the ladies' room at Bendel's. A dose of civility before boarding the five-fifty-seven up-line to Poughkeepsie, collecting the children, cooking, supping, homework, baths, the extended tucking-in ceremonies. "Mom, I know exactly who I want to be for Halloween," Erich would say every night, beginning in July.

"Good night, old man. Good night, little girl." So long ago. Not so long ago. What am I doing here without them? Why didn't all this happen fifteen or twenty years ago? Now I wash my face, change my shoes, trade my black linen shirt for a billowy white voile one. I put pearls in my ears. It is eventide in Venice and the sweet stranger loves pearls, so I add a necklace of them. Opium.

The forever barman at the Monaco is Paolo, dear Paolo, who had stuffed newspaper into my wet boots eight months before, when I'd missed my first rendezvous with Fernando. He herds us out onto the terrace into the luster of a slow-ripening evening. He brings us cold wine and says, *"Guardate.* Look," pointing with his chin at the mezzotint, the Canaletto, live before us in the rosy leavings of the sun.

His everyday tableau delights him, surprises him. Paolo can never be old in my eyes.

Across the canal sits a low-slung building, the maritime customs house of the republic's later days. The promontory is raised up above the lagoon on a million wooden pilings, and at the summit of the building's stone tower twin Atlases bear up a great golden sphere, a perch for Fortuna, goddess of all fates. She is beautiful. A timid wind tries to dance with her now. And slim shards of light become her. "*L'ultima luce.* Last light," we say to each other like a prayer. "Promise me we'll always be together at last light," Fernando says, needing no promise at all.

If I could give Venice to you for a single hour, it would be this hour, and it would be in this chair that I would sit you, knowing Paolo would be close by, clucking about over your comfort, knowing that the night that comes to thieve that lush *last light* would also make off with your heartaches. That's how it would be.

"Let's walk as far as Sant'Elena," he says. We cut through the piazza and head toward the Ponte della Paglia, past the Ponte dei Sospiri, onto the Riva degli Schiavoni, past the Danieli and another bridge, past a bronzed Vittorio Emmanuele on horseback, and another bridge in front of the Arsenale.

"How many more bridges?" I want to know.

"Only three. Then a boat from Sant'Elena to the Lido, a kilometer on foot to the apartment and we're there," he says. Nothing about this life is for the fainthearted.

After two days, Fernando goes off to the bank. I am kithless, my language is sparse and often contorted, and my groundings are only two: a kind of philosophic composure, that sense of "portable sanctuary," and my sweet stranger. I am free to begin coloring in that *crisp, new, just unrolled space* that appears to be my life.

Our joint plan is to confront a fundamental restoration of the apartment after the wedding. We will resurface walls and ceilings, hang new windows, completely reconstruct the bathroom and the kitchen, find furniture we love. For now, a swift ambient transformation with hard scrubbing and lots of fabric. Fernando tells me to rely on Dorina, his *donna delle pulizie,* cleaning woman. *Cleaning woman? What did she clean?*

Dorina arrives at eight-thirty on my first morning alone. Large, and long unbathed, she is a sixty-something woman who changes from her striped pinafore into another striped pinafore, which she carries in a wrinkled red shopping bag along with a pair of stacked-heel shoes, whose backs have been carved away. She moves about with a bucket of murky water, room to room with the same bucket of murky water and the same vile sponge. I ask Fernando if we might be able to find someone with more energy, but he refuses, saying Dorina has been with him for too many years. I like this loyalty to Dorina. The trick is only to keep her away from her bucket, to find something else for her to do, shopping, mending, ironing, dusting. I can finish the baptismal cleaning before she is due to return. I have thirteen days, and it's not exactly the *earth* I'm going to scrub. I can finish it in four, perhaps five. I think back to my evening chant in Saint Louis, *Weed, scrub, and dig clear down to China.*

Fernando helps by demonstrating the floor-polishing machine.

More a prototype for an upright motor scooter, it seems to me. Though its weight is light, I can't control its speed, and it has its way with me, jolting me about until I ask if a helmet is required to operate it. He doesn't think I'm funny. That neither he nor Dorina has ever had occasion to use it does not diminish the machine's status for him. "This represents the ultimate in Italian technology," says the churlish stranger. After it bucks him across the living room, we silently tuck the thing away, and I have never seen it since. Surely he sent Dorina home with it one day.

Next morning I splash vinegar-water everywhere and swab the floors with a new, green, string-headed mop. A splattering of pungent brown liquid from a tin labeled Marmi Splendenti, Resplendent Marbles, and I polish the floors by skating over them, my feet ensconced in the soft, felt envelopes Fernando wears as slippers. Under long, smooth glissades, the marbles give up a sheen. My thigh muscles burn. Though they are not truly resplendent, the floors' rusty-veined anthracite is beautiful to me, and I am eager to proceed. For Fernando it's not quite so. Each phase of the work causes him to grieve, before he shrugs into a temperate enthusiasm. We excavate the site, sifting things with anthropological sympathy, kneeling over moldering lockers and reproduction sea chests. In one I find a fifty-four piece audiocassette kit, its plastic coverings intact and labeled *Memoria e Metodo,* Memory and Method. It promises to "order one's mind."

"*Accidenti,*" he says. "Damn, I've searched everywhere for these." Each evening we relieve the apartment of another layer of its past, and Fernando's eyes are like those of a dying bird; his journeys to the trash dump are funeral. He is the one spurring on this interim cleanup, yet he is anguished by it. He desires progress without change.

I begin to establish survival rituals. As soon as Fernando leaves in the morning, I bathe and dress and, avoiding the elevator, run down the stairs, past the troll, out the gate, and to the left—fourteen yards to the yeast-perfumed, sugar-dusted threshold of Maggion. A tiny and glorious *pasticceria* whose resident pastry cook looks as a gingerbread man would look if he were a cherub. Inside it, I am near to a fever of joy. *This pastry shop is next door to my house,* I think. I take two apricot *cornetti,* crisp, burnished croissant-like beauties, and eat one on the way to the bar to drink cappuccino (fifty yards), the second on the way to investigate the *panificio,* the bakery (perhaps seventy yards, perhaps less), where I buy two hundred grams, not quite half a pound, of biscotti *al vino,* crisp cookies made with white wine and olive oil, fennel seeds, and orange peel. I tell myself these will be my lunch. In fact, they are to eat while I walk by the water, along a strip of sea-beaten sand that is the private beach of the Excelsior Hotel. Though Fernando assures me I can walk through its lobby, out its grand glass backdoors, and down to the sea without intervention, I prefer to swing my legs over the low stone wall of a terrace that looks to the water, edge my way down the embankment and onto the wet brown fringes of the Adriatic Sea. I am nearer yet to the fever. *The sea is across the street from my house,* I think. In summer and winter, in the rain, wrapped in furs, in a towel, once in a while in despair, I will walk this stretch of the Adriatic each day for three years of my life.

Back up the stairs to work, then back down the stairs two or three times more during the morning for espresso, for deep drafts of unmusty air, for one, maybe two, tiny strawberry tarts from the gingerbread cherub. Exits and reentries are recorded by the troll and her posse, each of whom is uniformed in a flower-printed smock. *Buon giorno* is all we say. I have lost hope for the welcoming black-stockinged lady, and I am less certain about the potency of tenderness and bitter chocolate. There is a stereo in the apartment but the only cassettes, besides *Memoria e Metodo,* are, of course, Elvis and Roy, and so I sing. I sing for the sheer joy of another beginning. How many houses have I made? I wonder. How many more will I make? Some people say that when your house is finished, it's time to die. My house is not finished.

By the third day, the scrubbing is nearly complete, and I'm ready to begin shopping. Fernando wants us to choose everything together, and so, when his workday ends, I'm there at the bank, and we go off to Jesurum for heavy ocher-colored sheets, a bedspread, a duvet, all dripping with eight inches of embroidered borders. We take masses of thick white towels and bath sheets adorned with milk chocolate-colored lace, a more intense ocher for an embossed damask tablecloth and napkins big as dish towels. These things are more expensive than a baby grand but, at last, there will be vanities in the stranger's lair.

Another day we buy a wonderful ivory lace coverlet in a *bottega* near Campo San Barnaba. Our treasure in hand, we walk a few yards round the corner to a sailing barge, a floating vegetable market, which, in one reincarnation or another, has rocked up along the Fondamenta Gherardini every day for seven or eight hundred years. We buy a kilo of peaches. Lace and peaches, the stranger's hand to hold. This is good. And it's this scene I think of as I crumple and fasten the lace to the overhead light fixture in the bedroom, stretching its edges taught and tying them to the posts of the headboard. Now we have a *baldacchino,* a canopied bed. Now we have a boudoir.

A vase of cobalt blue glass I find under the kitchen sink is gorgeous with branches of forsythia from the flower lady on the *imbarcadero,* boat landing. Once an extravagant ashtray, a large square dish of the same blue now holds artichokes nodding on thick long stems and lemons still attached to their leaves and twigs. Reine Claude plums, the color of new grass, are heaped in a basket carried from Madeira to New York to California to Missouri and, most recently, home here to Italy. Books line squeaky-clean glass shelves where once lived wounded model airplanes and tons of old pink newspapers, the *Gazzetta dello Sport.* I stand twenty or so photos in silver frames on the freshly beeswaxed and chammied lid of what seems to be a wonderful pine chest, a *cassapanca* he calls it. He says his father carted it down from Merano, the city that lies on the border with Austria, where the family once lived, where Fernando was born.

I will die with an unreformed and carnal love for fabric. Fabric matters more to me than furniture. Heirlooms and antiques aside, I'd rather drape and festoon some sorry, wounded relic than open the door to the Ethan Allen man. Shamelessly I head for the Lido market, which sets up on Wednesdays down by the canals. I buy a bolt of beige damask, lengths of which, unhemmed, warm up a black leather sofa. With a bolt of raw creamy silk I sort of gift-package the mismatched chairs, fashioning pouches for each one, tying them at their bases with silk cording. The glass and metal dining-room table is draped in a white linen bedspread, the ends of which are twisted into fat knots around its legs. A collection of Georgian candlesticks, rubbed, gleaming, I set like jewels in a row down its middle.

I find perfect poses for nearly every one of those old pillows I wouldn't leave behind in Saint Louis. All the surgery-efficient light-bulbs are replaced with *bugie*—literally, "lies"—low-wattage night lights and vanilla- and cinnamon-scented candles. Sunlight by day, candlelight in the evening: electricity can seem redundant. I am blithe while the stranger pouts.

Fernando is, in fact, livid when I show him the just-washed walls in the bedroom. He says walls in Venice can only be washed in autumn, when the air is relatively dry, or the dreaded black *muffa,* mold, will creep and crawl. Lord, as if it would matter, I think. We take turns on the ladder with my hair dryer.

He mourns the dead plants I set out on the terrace with the paint cans. *"Non sono morte, sono solo un po' addormentate.* They are not dead; they're just sleeping."

"You should know what *that's* like," I mutter sotto voce, carrying the plants back into the bedroom, trimming their crunchy leaves down to their sapless stalks. I begin finding how convenient it is to speak a language not understood by one's beloved. I stamp my feet hard through the apartment, flinging a wake of crushed leaves be-hind me and wondering why there always hovers, just an inch or two above love, some small itch for revenge.

A white rool rug from Sardinia conceals the ruins in the bath-room, and the red plastic-edged mirror over the sink is displaced by a smoked, beveled one fitted inside a baroque cornice from Gianni Cavalier in Campo Santo Stefano. He convinces us to buy two gold-leafed lily sconces to hang on either side of the mirror, even though

there are no outlets for them. "Attach them to the wall and put candles in them," he tells us, and that's what we do. Relieved of its
melancholy, the space is soft, inviting. We tell each other it feels
more like a country house or a cottage than an apartment. I begin
calling it "the dacha," and Fernando loves this. Now it seems a good
place to be, to eat and drink and talk, to think, to rest, to make love.
Fernando walks the space three, four times every day, surveying,
touching, half-smiling in a still-tentative approval.

Tingling with curiosity, the troll presses the buzzer one evening,
waving a piece of withheld mail to secure her entry. *"Posso dare un oc-
chiata?* May I take a quick look?"

Her twitterings please Fernando. *"Ma qui siamo a Hollywood. Brava,
signora, bravissima. Auguri, tanti auguri.* Here we are in Hollywood.
Good, signora, very good. Good wishes, many good wishes," she
says, scuttling back down the stairs. The bunker will be informed by
midnight. Thanks to the troll I begin to understand that Fernando
needs endorsement, confirmation, before he can embrace what I
do. If I can please the crowd, he is pleased. Seven years later, three
houses later, as I am telling you this now, still he waits for a testi-
monial, maybe two, before relaxing into approval.

Rallied then, Fernando begins to summon neighbors and colleagues to stop by for a peek at the place. No one is asked to sit, to
drink a glass of wine. Each one knows his office is to reconnoiter and
report to the rest of the island. I am part of the furniture, a parlor
chair upholstered in vintage Norma Kamali, and no one speaks directly to me. Addressing the air eight inches above my head, one of
them might come forth with some flummery like, *"Signora, Le piace
Venezia?* Does the lady like Venice?" Then, in a sort of mechanized

minuet, he turns smartly around and out the door. I will learn that this is a form of Venetian social life, that some of these "visitors" will wax affectionately for years about what a lovely time they passed in our home. Nothing feels real yet, and I begin wondering if it ever will. More, I begin wondering if I will remember what *real* is, should it resurface. I play house. It's a little like when the children were babies and I could play dolls. But no, this is different. Then I was much older.

Though he's on his own turf, doing the things he has done always, Fernando, too, has slid through the looking glass. He walks up and down the same avenues, says *buona sera* to the same people, buys his cigarettes from the same tobacconist, gulps the same *aperitivo* in the same bar where he's gulped it for thirty years, yet now, nothing is the same. Fernando has his own stranger. "You, too, are inside another life," I say to him.

He says no. He says this is not another life but a first life. "At least the first life where I've been anything more than an observer," he says. There is a bittersweetness in my stranger. And a long-repressed hot tremor of anger. I think how lonely it would be to just bump along, to hang on, while life drives one about. I believe in the fates, in a kind of fundamental predestination, but fused with home-cured strategy. I remember, when I was still very young, feeling relieved, reading Tolstoy. "Life will shape itself," he promised. Though I didn't buy it completely, I was so happy to think life might do even a part of its own work, that I could rest once in a while. But to sleep as Fernando had slept was sad.

It's a Saturday evening and, with no aim, we float. Out on the deck of a vaporetto I pull Prosecco from my purse; the wine, having

rested an hour or so in the freezer, is achingly cold, its tight sharp
bubbles an anesthetic on the tongue. He is timid, hoping no one will
mistake him for a tourist, but he takes long hard pulls of the wine.
*"Hai sempre avuto una borsa così ben fornita?* Have you always had such
a well-stocked purse?" he asks. My purse is an evolved diaper bag,
I explain. I *try* to explain. We have already taken to speaking a hybrid
of our languages, a sort of homemade Esperanto. Or sometimes he
will ask a question in English and I will answer in Italian. Each wants
the other's comfort. The boat plunges through black water, through
wet, silky air shot with a pink light that becomes amber before it becomes gold.

On the Zattere we debark, change boats, and ride back to San
Zaccaria. It's nearly nine. Curiously few strangers are about and, in
the sultry air, the piazza drowses. Our steps sound hollow as violins
send Vivaldi and Frescobaldi back and forth from the cafés across the
unpeopled space. There is no one to dance, and so *we* dance. We
dance even when there is no music, until some boisterous Germans
on their way to supper begin to dance along with us. *"Sei radiosa,"*
Fernando says. "You are radiant. You wear Venice very well. It's rarely
so, even among Venetians and, as for foreigners, they are most often
ignored, obscured by her. Foreigners are mostly invisible in Venice.
You are not invisible," he says softly and almost as though it would be
easier for him if I were.

We decide to have supper at Il Mascaron in Santa Maria Formosa,
a place that had always been my favorite during earlier Venice trips.
I love angling up to the slab of old wood that is its bar, demijohns of
Refosco and Prosecco and Torbolino crowding the space. Gigi
heaves down tumblersful of Tokay, fizzy and white-capped from its

fast tense journey through the spigot. We tell him what we'd like for antipasti from white oval dishes of *baccalà mantecato, castraure, sarde in saor, fagioli bianchi con cipolle,* codfish mousse, thumbnail-sized artichokes, sardines in sour sauce, white beans with onions. Ancient, sharp, sensual. Canonical Venice from the tines of a fork.

As we head back to the boat, the air now is drenched in darkening blue. I feel a shivery reckoning. *This is my neighborhood.* I am giddy, weepy, and yet—as though it has always been mine, as though all of this has always been mine—I am easy inside this happiness. I trust this happiness. But Mr. Quicksilver, whose moods are always changing, breaks through the peace.

When I ask about one palazzo or another, about an artist, an era, he answers indifferently or not at all, a reluctant guide. "Venice is not exotic to Venetians," he says. "And besides, I don't know all the answers. There are parts of the city where I have never been. I want you to know me first, to be at home with me, and then we'll worry about helping you to feel at home with *her,*" he says like a jealous lover. "You're not here on vacation, you know," he continues.

*Vacation,* I want to scream. *Do you have any recollection how I've spent these past weeks?* I want to scream louder, looking down at my two-hundred-year-old hands. I would be able to scream these words only in English, and I already know he would dart behind incomprehension even if he understood every bloody syllable.

"I can't find anything in my own house. I reach for a pair of scissors and there are no scissors," he says with the now familiar dead-bird eyes.

"I don't even *have* a house," I remind him, saying the words as diabolically as I dare. I'm on a roll now, and I don't care if he understands. I'm going to say how I feel, and I'm going to say it in my own language. "I have no equilibrium, no job. And what about a friend? How about someone, anyone, looking me in the eye and saying welcome. What about a clean glass?" I seethe out.

We walk a little more before he stops again and, wearing the moon and the beginnings of a smile, as though we'd just taken turns reading to each other from *Bread and Jam for Frances,* he says, "Tell me what I can do to make you feel *at home.*" It's my turn not to answer. Revenge flutters nearby.

# 7

# That Lush Moment Just Before Ripeness

Slowly, very slowly, I begin to feel I *am* at home. Sometimes I step out-of-scene for a moment, checking to see if I find some shabby sense of farce about us. Are we used people pretending to be new? No. The most stringent pulse-taking always reads negative. We are not old. We are at that lush moment just before ripeness, the moment that love suspends in a soft, sustained note of rhapsody. In the cinnamon candlelight and a lengthening tenderness, we strangers live well together in the little dacha. As a couple there is some sense about us that feels like risk, like adventure, like the tight, sharp bubbles of a good Prosecco. Even when we bewilder each other, make each other screaming crazy, there's a bright metal ring to us like the resonance of something gold and something silver tumbling fast across wet stones. It feels as if we're living on the eve of a rapture.

The stranger likes me to tell him stories. One evening, stretched out on the sofa, his head in my lap, he says, "Tell me about the very first time you saw Venice."

"You know that story," I groan.

"I don't know *all* of the story. Tell me everything. You were with a man, right?" he sits up and looks at me.

"I was not with a man, and what if I was?" I half taunt.

But he's serious, gentle. "Please just tell me the story."

"Okay. But close your eyes and really listen, because it's a beautiful story. Try not to fall asleep," I say.

"You know the part about my being in Rome, about my not wanting to leave Rome to go to Venice. But I had an assignment to write about Venice and so I *had* to go. Do you remember all of that?" I ask placing the event like a good *raconteuse*.

"Yes. I remember you arrived by train and that you debarked at San Zaccaria so you could listen for la Marangona,"

"Which never rang," I interrupt.

"Which never rang. But why didn't you walk in the piazza then? How could you be right there at the entrance and then turn away?" he asks sitting up again so he can read my face. He lights a cigarette in the candle flame, walks across the living room and opens the doors to the little terrace. Stepping outside, he leans against the railing, facing me, waiting.

"I don't know, Fernando. I just wasn't ready. I wasn't ready for how Venice made me feel, from that first moment when I walked out through the doors of the train station. It was as though Venice was more than a place. It was as though Venice was a person, someone familiar but not familiar at all, someone who caught me off guard. I was pretty jaded back then. I'd already been many places, seen so much, I just wasn't prepared for the frenzy of emotions in that moment," I tell him.

"Just as you were unprepared when you first met me?" he asks.

"Yes. Very much as I was when I first met you," I say. "Now come back and lie down and close your eyes so I can tell you the story."

Fernando takes his position.

*Map in hand, I head for a place called Il Gazzettino, the small hotel chosen for me by my editors. I find Campo San Bartolomeo easily enough and then follow the crush left onto the narrow, dark path of the Merceria, pushing and pulling my suitcase down the alleyways.*

"Campo San Bartolomeo? You walked right past the door of the bank," he says, as though the motion was deliberate disrespect.

"Be quiet and keep your eyes closed," I tell him.

*I open the door to a tiny, empty reception hall and tug at the bell on the wall. Il Gazzettino, whose décor I later came to know as travestied Venetian, is done almost entirely in Murano glass—chandeliers and vases and sculptures of lurid form and color cover every surface of it except those where prints of lascivious, mocking carnevale figures hang. The light is murky. I begin to miss Rome again. Through the door behind me bursts in a small, smiling woman called Fiorella, she tells me, as she tucks the great, wretched bag under her arm and carries it off up the stairs. My room is outfitted in the house theme and, in defense, I drape a lacy shawl over the worst of the grinning harlequins. The grotesqueness of the space dissolves in the light from the single window that opens onto the backstreet Venetian pageant of the Sottoportego de le Acque. I hoist myself up onto the windowsill and lean back against the frame of the thick, black shutters and sit for a while, breathing in the scene. I applaud the old basso serenading from a gondola in the rio below, and he bows deeply from the waist, as though the tipsy little boat was a prop on the stage at la Fenice. The light goes to shadows, and I feel a little* cold. Back inside, I dance round the room like a boxer, not knowing how to begin to wrap my arms around Venice. And what about supper? Shall I go now to see the piazza or wait until dark? I decide to wash my hair and change clothes, then wander about the neighborhood in search of my sea legs and a good aperitivo.

I tie up my hair, slide into a sheath made from a length of saffron-colored silk I'd bought years before in Rome, originally intending it to be a skirt for my dressing table. It's a pretty dress, I think, as I buckle my gray snakeskin sandals. I am going to walk in Venice.

"Do you still have that dress?" he wants to know.

"No. I gained weight and it didn't fit anymore, so I made pillow covers out of it. And if you interrupt once more, I'm going to bed," I promise.

Fiorella counsels that I should wait for tomorrow to begin searching out the more typical places to eat and drink and that I should stay close by, round the corner at Antico Pignolo. I was to learn that Fiorella prevails. She phones up the Pignolo, books a table, severely recommends their kind treatment of me, and tells me to return immediately upstairs to change my shoes—all before I can begin to protest. I pretend not to understand about the shoes and race out into a sheer watered-silk twilight.

Once more defying Fiorella, I walk quickly—again, as though to an appointment—up the Merceria to Calle Fiubera, over Calle dei Barcaroli and Calle del Fruttarol and out into Campo San Fantin. Outside the Taverna della Fenice I sit sipping cold Prosecco and feeling a strange sort of consolation. Some balmy caress from the wine, from the sweet, wet air on my skin? The old Princess provokes a shivery farawayness in me. And yet I do not feel out of place; I feel oddly at home. I drift more than I walk on the return, *stopping, peering into angles, touching the worn surface of a wall or a great brass lion's head guarding a small palace and masquerading as a door knocker. I am beginning to understand the rhythmic game of capture and release one can play with Venice. Light into shadow and back into light, amid her musty, pinched alleys I drift. As I have sometimes drifted through life. And so it is sheepish and starving that I arrive an hour and a half late for my table.*

Fernando interrupts, "And after dinner did you go to San Marco?"

"Yes," I say.

*I come through the Piazzetta dei Leoncini and look, full-face, into the piazza. A long, broad moonlit ballroom it seems, with the brooding domes of the basilica its portal. The walls are grand arches flounced in white canvas; its floor is stone smoothed by rains and lagoon waters and a thousand years of the strolling, dancing, marching feet of fishermen and courtesans, of white-breasted noblewomen, of old doges and hungry children, of conquerors and of kings. There are a few people walking, a few more sit outside at Quadri. It is from Florian that the music comes. The ensemble plays "Weiner Blut," and two couples of a certain age dance unselfconsciously. I take a table near them and stay there, sipping American coffee, until there is no one left dancing or sitting or playing a violin. I leave lire on the table so as not to disturb the huddle of waiters taking off their ties and lighting one another's cigarettes. I am unsure of the way back to the horrid little room over the Sottoportego de le Acque, but it is only a few mistaken turns onto silent calli before I find Fiorella's hotel.*

*One day I ride out to Torcello to walk in the long meadow grasses and rest in the seventh-century dimness of Santa Maria dell'Assunta. I sit under the pergola at Osteria al Ponte del Diavolo to eat risotto with hop shoots, served by a waiter with pomaded hair parted in the middle and a salmon-colored silk cravat.*

"Where we ate on your first weekend here," says Fernando.

*I see dozens of churches and the sublime paintings that hide in some of them, never setting foot inside the Accademia or the Correr during that first visit. My research of the* bacari, *wine bars, is rather intermittent and spontaneous. As I come across one, I stop in and sip Incrocio Manzoni or a tumbler of Malbec or of Recioto, always with some sort of wonderful* cicheti, *appetizers. I like the barely hard-boiled halves of eggs, their yolks orange and soft and ornamented with a sliver of fresh sardine and the tiny fried octopus dressed in oil, thumbnail-sized artichokes in a garlicky bath. I find it easy, really, to avoid the Venice of which I had been so long diffident. She presents a clear choice between stepping into or away from cliché. Her heart's blood rushes just beneath her artifice. Just like mine, I think. Venice wants only a little pluck as the price of entry onto her sentimental routes.*

I don't know how long he'd been sleeping, why I never noticed the quiet clicking of his snore. Anyway, I was happy for the chance to have heard my story. Carefully I walk him to bed, thinking he is gone for the night, but, once there, he props himself up on his elbows, "Will you tell me *everything* tomorrow night?"

The stranger has less trouble staying awake for our baths. And early on we find our best talking takes place in the tub. For two people so full of mysteries as we are, there is a spiritual intimacy between us that needs no coaxing. As it was from that first evening in Saint Louis, I'm the bath maker. I pour in handfuls of green tea salts and sandalwood oil, too much foaming pine, and a drop or two of musk. I always make the water too hot, and I'm always submerged among the bubbles and steam when Fernando enters the bathroom. He lights the candles. It takes him a full four minutes to adjust to the water as his pale skin blooms crimson. *"Perché mi fai bollire ogni volta?* Why do you wish to boil me each time?"* During one bath time the subject is cruelty. I want to tell him more about my first marriage.

I open with, "I betrayed my first husband. He was a patient man who waited for me to provide a clear-cut reason so he could leave me. He couldn't just say, I don't love you, I don't want this marriage, or you, or these children. He told me these things only many years later. At the time, what he did was to reinforce my clearly pathological insecurities about being a lovable person.

"He's a psychologist. He's also cunning. And what he did was stop talking to me. He withdrew, leaving me to stumble and tremble, to wonder what was happening. And when he did talk, mostly it was to ridicule and threaten. He seemed to enjoy his immense capacity to frighten me." Fernando's face is no longer red but very white. Each phrase seems to need five minutes of translation, then another eternity for him to take it in. At least the water is cooling. But I'm crying.

I continue, "I didn't even understand what depression was, but depressed I must have been. I was pregnant with Erich during the worst of it. Perhaps I knew then that his father was already gone from us. It was my little girl, Lisa, who got excited by the baby's first kick. It was she, her head in my lap, who rejoiced at his rumblings, translated them for me. She and I sang to the baby, told him how we already loved him, that we couldn't wait to hold him. Still, somehow, Erich was born knowing about sadness."

Now Fernando is crying too, and he says he needs me to be in his arms, and so we slosh out to the bedroom and lie down.

"Soon after Erich's birth, there were moments when I confronted my husband, telling him I was lonely and frightened. 'Why are you so cruel,' I'd ask him. 'Why don't you hold your daughter? Why don't you hold the baby? Why don't you love us?'

"But he was just biding his time waiting for that exit cue. So I provided it, Fernando, I provided just the perfect reason to make him go away. I met a man and fell madly for him. I thought him kind and sensitive. I saw him infrequently, but I was certain his passion was an expression of love. 'Ah, so this is what it's like,' I'd think. When my husband followed my well-laid tracks, I still believed he'd fight for me. But he was gone in three days. Still it would be okay because the other man really loved me. He really loved me, I was sure.

"I couldn't tell my lover by telephone, though, so I got on the train and we met for lunch and I said, 'He knows. He knows everything, and now he's gone and we're free.'

"'Free to do what?' he asked me, without taking the cigarette from his mouth.

"'Free to be together. I mean, that's what you want, isn't it?' I asked him. He was a master at hesitation. Through a fresh puff of smoke, I heard him say, 'Fool.' He must have said other things, but that's all I can remember. I got up from my chair and careened to the ladies' room. I stayed there, being sick, for a very long time. The woman who tended the rest room was waiting for me when I finally came out of the toilet, a wet cloth in her hand. She told me to lean on her, to sit. I tried to laugh, saying that perhaps I was pregnant. 'No. This is a broken heart,' she told me. The French say that women die only from the first man. For me, death came twice in the same week."

We lay there quietly until Fernando got up on his knees and, looking down at me, his hands on my shoulders, he said, "There isn't an agony in this world more powerful than tenderness."

# 8

# Everyone Cares How They Are Judged

*A*s often as I give the stranger reasons to cry, I seem to give him even more reasons to laugh. I tell his colleague at the bank, a man from Pisa, that I find *i piselli* among the kindest folks in Italy. Unfortunately what I really say is that I find *peas* to be among the kindest folks in Italy. *Piselli,* peas. The citizens of Pisa are called *pisani.* Signor Muzzi is clever enough to not react to my gaffe and loquacious enough to recount and embroider the story so that *l'americana* causes tittering among staff and clients.

Unembarrassed, I am happy to have caused this burlesque. Concentrating so much on day-by-day rejoicing, I hardly notice the malaise that is settling on me: a suggestion of sadness, a bruise that comes and goes and returns, nostalgia. This feeling is not tragic, nor does it contradict the fullness of this new life. It is mainly that I miss my own language. I miss the *sounds* of English. I want to *understand and be understood.* Of course, I know the salves. Apart from time itself, there is the English-speaking community, members of which are dispersed all over Venice. I need a chum. And perhaps there is something else: I miss my own ebullience.

I feel squeezed by this northern stance of *bella figura,* the keeping of the façade, the quick strangling of spontaneity for the sake of a necessary deception that Italians call "elegance." It prescribes a short list of approved questions and answers. Fernando is my *scu-diero,* my shield bearer, protecting himself and me from "foul whisperings." Whenever we are in public he moves about mincingly, trying to distract me from cultural mortification. It's no use. Too often I feel like a middle-aged Bombastes with very red lips. Unimpressed by, insensitive to my own blunderings, I talk to everyone. I am curious, I smile too much, touch and peer and inspect. It seems the stranger and I are comfortable only when we're alone together.

"*Calma, tranquilla,*" he says to me, the generic warning against every behavior that is not short-listed. Archaic posturing among people who seem to care less than a fig about each other—this nonverbal patois is their real language, and I cannot speak it. It was just as Misha had said it would be.

Born and bred in Russia, Misha had emigrated to Italy as a newly graduated medical doctor and worked in Rome and Milan for nearly ten years before settling in America. He and I first met when we both lived in New York. We became closer friends after he transferred to Los Angeles and I was up in Sacramento. Misha always had lots to say. He came to visit me in Saint Louis just after I'd met Fernando and our first lunch together was long and angry.

"Why are you doing this? What is it you want from this man? He has none of the obvious merits women are likely to race across the earth to cling to," he said in his Rasputin voice. He went on about the perils of exchanging cultures, about how I would be surrendering even the simple joy of discourse. "Even when you learn to truly think and speak in another language, it is not the same as engaging in native fluency. You will neither *understand nor be understood.* That's always been so fundamental to you. You who love words, who say wonderful things in that small, soft voice. There will be no one to hear you," he said. Though it was clear this was a soliloquy, I tried to jump in.

"Misha, I'm in love for the first time in my life. Is it then improbable that I would want to be with this man whether he lives in El Paso or Venice?" I asked. "I'm not choosing a culture. I'm choosing a lover, a partner, a husband." He was ruthless.

"But who will you be there, what will you be able to do? The Mediterranean culture in general and the Italian culture in particular operate on a different standard of impressions and judgments. You're not nineteen, you know, and the best they'll think about you is that you 'must have once been a beauty.' It will be important if you can make them think you have money, which you don't. Nothing else much will matter. This is an eccentric sort of move you are making and most will be wary of you and ask, 'What is it she wants here?' It is inconceivable for them even to consider purity of motive because they contrive so. Every move is staged to effect a countermove. I don't suggest this is singularly Italian, but I do suggest that the intensity of this sort of posturing is as rampant there today as it was in the Middle Ages. Clever as you are, you'll still be too childlike for them. There's too much of Pollyanna in you for their tastes. That you are an eternal beginner, if that can be contemplated at all, will seem frivolous to them. Better that your Fernando were a rich old arthritic bastard. Then they might understand your attraction to him," he pounded.

"Misha, why can't you simply acknowledge my happiness, even be happy for me?" I asked.

"Happy—what is 'happy'? Happiness is for stones, not for

people. Every once in a while our lives are illuminated by something or someone. We get a flash and we call it 'happiness.' You are behaving spontaneously, and yet you will be judged contrarily because you can only be judged by their standards, which do not embrace spontaneity," he concluded slowly, deliberately.

"I don't care how I'm judged," I said.

"Everyone cares how they are judged," he said.

I'd tried to listen to him back then, but mostly I'd tucked away his gloom as though looking at it would make me feel foolish and frightened. And bringing his gloom forward now does make me feel foolish and frightened.

Timidly, Fernando begins to introduce me to one person or another whom we happen upon in the street, on the ferry boat or the vaporetto, at the newsstand on Sunday mornings or when we stop to drink an Aperol at Chizzolin or to sit at Tita over iced metal cups of *gelato di gianduia*. On the weekends we drive out toward Alberoni, stopping at Santin to take the island's best coffee, to eat warm pastries stuffed with rum and chocolate, and later in the evening, when the place is even more crowded, we go again for crisp little ricotta tarts and flutefuls of Prosecco. But this is a place where no one really wants to talk with anyone else. Either people are alone and they like it that way or they come to perform, to talk *at* the crowd. And as the bar goes, so goes the island. I will learn that those Lidensi whom he called his friends were nearly all "five-phrase" companions, their affection demonstrated in chance meetings with discourse that opens on the weather and closes with airy kisses and a promise to call. But no one ever calls anyone on the Lido.

Usually, the whole stiff ambience makes me smile. It's a bad *Mr.*

*Roger's Neighborhood* episode, and I comfort the little hurts that it sometimes inflicts by remembering it isn't *his island,* anymore than it is his house for which I'd come to live with Fernando. I take to composing little songs, teaching them to him in English so that, at the least, we can poke fun at the perfect precision of each encounter. He likes this, wickedly enlarges upon it. But if I dare protest some particularly bewildering response or event, he perceives aggression and changes flags, haughtily defending his island. "But who do you think you are that you can judge or try to change a culture? *Quanto pomposa sei.* How pompous you are."

I try to tell him that I don't mean to judge. I'm not trying to change anything about these people or their culture. I am only try-ing not to have to change anything about myself or mine. He can seem some holograph image, a stranger, fading and finding form, fading and finding form. Is Fernando's journey away from the *bella figura,* which he will freely tell you he detests, just too new? One step forward, many steps backward. Even now—right now—that the road behind him is long, still he dances the old dances. And I dance mine.

And when he is neither defending the Lido nor making a meal of the place, Fernando tells me stories of how it used to be here, how, until the early sixties, the Gran Viale was banked in swanky sidewalk tea rooms with morning-coated waiters and string quartets where Austrian and French soubrettes lingered in hats with veils, their con-sorts in crumpled white linen suits. I am forty years too late. Now there are only taverns with pizza ovens. The only exotics I see on the avenue are sun-seekers from Düsseldorf in short shorts and plastic sandals. And the only person with a hat is me. Except for the brief postwar civility of the tea rooms, nothing much had happened on the Lido since Byron, in short pants, was wont to charge a chestnut stallion into its waves, dive into the lagoon, and backstroke through the blue-green waters of the Grand Canal.

Everyone with some place to run escapes the Lido in boats each day, as though it were the tenth circle of hell, while those who remain are condemned to swift survival forays into the shops, then back behind the shutters for daytime sleeps and television vigils. Despite the shortcomings of this island, I keep trying to find the chocolate side of the Lido. In some ways this seems easy to me because it is surrounded by the sea—*I* am surrounded by the sea; pieces of its beach are like other rooms in my house. It loosens the sun in the morning and lures it back beneath its bosom at night. But even the sea, with its sulks and tempers and complexions, cannot rouse this sandy little fiefdom from its torpor. Although there is the beach ladies' dance.

Until now, I'd spent less than a total of forty minutes of my life actually lying still under a hot burning sun. Here, I live in a culture that mandates all females roast their skin. I didn't even own a bathing suit. Once the dacha, as we continue to call the apartment, is in order, I go off to Milan to exchange some papers with the American consulate and to buy an Alaia, bias-cut, one-piece, beautiful. If I can't *be* an Italian, at least I will *look* like one. Tied up in a white pareo, shaded in Versace, a pearly pink mouth sealing my disguise, I wait until ten (beach ladies don't rise early), walk across the street, this time sashaying straight through the sanctum of the Excelsior Hotel and out to the sands. There waits hell's eleventh circle.

Women lie in the sun and smoke in front of their cabanas for three hours in the morning, sleep for two hours at home after lunch, return to the beach to lie in the sun and smoke for three hours in the afternoon, until their husbands join them at six-thirty for *aperitivi* at the hotel bar. Still at the beach, they shower, with a cigarette pinched between their lips; they dress with a cigarette pinched between their lips, and, smoking still, they go off to dinner. She, with skin like a crinkled russet leaf and weighted by a kilo of gold and jewels, seems more exhausted than he. The bathing suit goes to live in the bottom drawer of my bureau.

Beach life archived, I think about cooking. In the few weeks that have passed, we've mostly supped early and modestly, in little *osterie* in Venice after I meet Fernando each evening at the bank. Sometimes we've gone home to change clothes before carting a basket of bread and cheese and wine and chocolates down to the seaside rocks for a ten o'clock picnic. But tonight, Fernando will sup at home.

I set off on foot across Ponte delle Quattro Fontane onto Via Sandro Gallo on my way to the *quartiere popolare*—the working-class neighborhood on the Lido where Fernando says I'll find better things less expensively than in the shops nearby. This is perhaps true, but it is also true that long lengths of hot, sun-licked avenue lie between each merchant. I make visits to the dairyman, the butcher, the fishmonger, the fruitman (who is different from the vegetable man, who is different from the herb seller). Flour, olive oil, pancetta from the *gastronomia*. I, the newly arrived Philistine, ask for *lievito,* yeast, at the bakery. With round eyes the baker's wife says she does not sell yeast, she sells bread. She says the bread is baked at the *forno,* oven, which is located at the other end of the island. Her post is only a dispensary. Does she know where I can find yeast, I ask. Yeast for cakes? Baking powder? It is this you desire, no? she tests me. "No, signora, yeast for baking bread," I say. My intentions cause her chest to heave. I buy bread to diffuse her agony. I forgo the *pasticceria,* only a few hundred yards further on and recommended by the wine seller, giving thanks for the nearness of Maggion. Half a day later, muscles twitching from the weight of sacks hauled three miles and up three flights of stairs, I am sunburnt, triumphant, and ready to begin.

Heretofore I have lit the stove only to brew coffee. I discover that the burner I'd been using is the only one that functions, the others wooshing out mostly air. The single window is sealed shut, and the twelve square inches of floor space invite only a discreet sort of sway-ing from the waist up. Except one for prepping grapefruit, there are no knives, and it seems mine fell among the goods given away at the airport. I think about the hundreds of cooking classes I've taught, my bantering on the subject of a well-equipped home kitchen. I hear my sassy self telling the students, "Adequate space, fine tools, and equipment are fundamental. But if one is really a cook, one can cook in a tin can with a wooden spoon." I was wrong. I need more than a tin can, and much more than this tin-can-of-a-space. And dammit, I need more than a wooden spoon.

Still, I make a batter for enormous golden squash blossoms and stuffing for a veal breast with pistachios and pancetta and Parmesan and sage. Plumped and tied up in cotton string, I braised the veal in butter and white wine and I let it rest and cool in its pan juices. There will be an iced soup of roasted yellow tomatoes adorned with a pair of anise-grilled prawns to begin, a wedge of Taleggio—ripe, runny—white figs, and meringues from Maggion at the finish. We dine slowly. Fernando is curious about each dish, wanting to know components and methods. He asks how long it has taken me to prepare the supper, and I tell him it took three times longer to shop than to cook.

"You mustn't think I expect you to set a table like this each evening," he says. I wonder if he is saying, You mustn't expect me to *eat* like this each evening. Sure enough he continues, "I prefer *simplicity*. Besides," he continues, "you have so much to do, a wedding to plan, the renovation to oversee, a language to learn." I understand. There is a detour on the way to his heart that totally evades his stomach.

"But I'm a cook. You can't just tell me not to cook," I wail.

"I'm not telling you not to cook," he tells me through his teeth. "What I'm saying is that your idea of everyday cooking is my idea of festival cooking," he says, as though festival cooking is profane.

Why is it so peculiar that I want to *cook, really cook, every day?* He thinks that once, perhaps, twice a week seems more correct. Other nights we could eat a simple *pasta asciutta* or a salad and some cheese, *prosciutto e melone, mozzarella e pomodoro.* We could go to eat pizza. He persists. The kitchen is so small, so *unprepared* for serious cooking, he says. It is he who is *unprepared* for serious eating, I think. That I would bake bread terrifies him more than it did the baker's wife.

"No one bakes bread or desserts or makes pasta at home," he says. "Even grandmothers and maiden aunts queue in the shops rather than cook and bake." We are a *modern culture,* he tells me over and over again. On the Lido this means that women have been liberated from the kitchen into the *salotto* to watch television and play canasta,

I think. "We have some of the finest *artigiani* in all Italy who make these things so we don't have to make them," he says. Next he's going to tell me on which days the Bo-Frost truck passes by the bunker, that icy provider of the beach ladies' lunch, the ever ready purveyor of perfectly rectangular foods. I wince, but he does not propose the Bo-Frost solution.

Throughout these discourses I know he means well, that he wants only to help me adjust to the new realities. There are no longer forty hungry guests who would come to supper each evening as they had at the café. There are no children, no extended family to sit at our table. And Fernando has already told me that here friends and neighbors eat at their own tables. I feel like the Little Red Hen in menopause. This will all pass, as soon as the wedding is over, the apartment properly renovated, the weather cooler. The stranger will be hungry and, from somewhere, I would collect a few takers for supper once in a while. I'll get a job in a restaurant. I'll open my own restaurant. If I'd had my knives, I would have thrown them down. Fernando pulls me up from my silent anger by tartly announcing, "Tomorrow evening, I'll cook for you." I can't wait, I think sourly. Later, in bed, I plot how to better present my culinary self to the stranger.

I had spent nearly twenty years working with food, dreaming about it, writing about it, teaching other people how to work with it, chasing it over far-flung continents, paying the rent for a well-lived life with the often considerable spoils gleaned from a career based on it, a career he thinks to have been a *jobette,* a very nice sort of paid hobby. I'd been the trusted architect of others' as well as my own gastronomically fired dreams. More than once I'd bet the farm and kept it, relying on what I knew and felt about food. I will say all this quietly and over time. I will even pull out my scruffy briefcase full of printed testimony, saved over the years from magazines and newspapers. But when I do, all the stranger has to offer is, "Now that you are 'without language,' you think the way to communicate is with food." Prattle.

For me, food is far beyond the metaphors for love and sentiment and "communication." I do not demonstrate affection with food. Less noble than that, I cook because *I* love to cook, because *I* love to eat, and if someone is near who also loves to eat, all the better. The truth is I have always cooked for crowds, even when there were no crowds—for the crowds I, always and still, *wished* there to be. My children say I once made a pumpkin soup, that I roasted a surfeit of jack-o'-lanterns into caramelized softness, mixed the flesh with cognac and cream and a few scrapings of nutmeg. There were gallons of it, they say. After a week's worth of suppers, they watched me add shreds of Emmenthaler and just-cracked white pepper and egg yolks to what was left. They say I folded in whites whipped to stiffness and turned the mass into buttered, crumbed molds, three very large molds, they say. *Voilà,* savory pudding. I remember that it was wonderful, even on the second and third nights. Lisa will tell you it was then that her skin began to turn orange. In the end I scooped what was left of the pudding into a work bowl with some ricotta and a few tablespoonsful of grated Parmesan and made gnocchi: pumpkin gnocchi with sage butter and roasted pumpkin seeds is how *their* story ends, though *I* remember one more night in the great pumpkin episode. Yes, I'm sure we had those gnocchi, at least once, au gratin with cream and tiny dollops of Gorgonzola. Plenty from spoils. It is naive, perhaps, but all this suits me, this pull toward domestication. This is the oldest thing I know about myself, the first thing, really. Except for the loneliness.

The next evening the stranger stands by the stove like the duke of Montefeltro, in purple silk boxers. Bringing out a balance, he measures 125 grams of pasta, for each of us. I am going to marry a Venetian J. Alfred Prufrock who measures out his supper in grams! He pours tomato puree into a small, thin, beat-up old pan rather than one of my little copper beauties. He adds salt and big pinches of dried herbs that he kept in a tin on top of the stove. *"Aglio, peperoncino, e prezzemolo.* Garlic, chili, and parsley," he says, as though he believes it. The pasta is good, and I tell him so, but I am still hungry.

Three hours later I am hollow with that hunger and so, when Fernando falls asleep, I creep out of bed and cook a whole pound of fat, thick spaghetti. I drench it with butter scented with a few drops of the twenty-five-year-old balsamic vinegar that I'd carried, coddled like a Fabergé egg, from Spilamberto to Saint Louis to Venice. I grate a wedge of Parmesan over the pasta until my hand gets tired and then ornament the silky, steamy mass with long grindings of pepper. I raise the shutters in the dining room to let in moonlight and midnight breezes, light a candle, and pour wine. Serving myself over and over again, I devour the pasta, I absorb it, smelling, tasting, chewing, feeling the comfort of it explode again and again. Revenge flutters, and so I twirl it rebelliously, round and round on my fork exactly the way Fernando told me not to twirl it. Finally Lucullus has dined with Lucullus.

I sit there, exhausted, one hunger sated, the next hunger bristling. Fernando can eat like Prufrock till the end of time if that pleases him, but I'm going to cook and I'm going to eat like me. What was it he called me, *pomposa?* Just look at who's being pompous? I've sat still for more "suggestions," counsel, and downright direction during this past month than I had during my whole life. He doesn't like my clothes, he doesn't like my *modo d'essere,* my style of being, he doesn't like my cooking. My skin is too white, my mouth too large. Maybe he did fall in love with a profile instead of with me. I feel like I've drunk the potion from the wrong little vial. Fernando is diminishing me, erasing me. And I have indulged him.

Smiling through the process, I have been trying to honor the old pact I'd made with myself about understanding his need to lead. But I never made a pact about even the softest form of tyranny. I know he believes he is helping me. Perhaps he even sees himself as my Svengali, a kind of savior. Have I been so agreeable because I fear discord will turn him away? The *fresh, just unrolled space* of this new life, am I trying to color it in too perfectly? Am I trying to compensate for what I'm still holding onto as sentimental failures so he won't leave me, too? There is so much that is beautiful about loving Fernando and being loved by him, but I miss myself. I loved me so much more as a woman than I do as a withering moppet in demure surrender. I will not stay on this island nor in this house, courting the local unconsciousness. Culinary or otherwise, I tell myself, patting my happy, turgid belly. I prefer to link up with the fugitives who ride over the water to Venice each morning than to stay napping with the anchorites. I clear away all traces of my sins and slip back into bed. The stranger never hears my crying.

# 9

# Have You Understood that These Are the Earth's Most Beautiful Tomatoes?

Next morning I am resolved to wake up the sleeping voluptuary in me. After packing the stranger off to the bank with the empty briefcase he insists on carrying everywhere, I race about the apartment scraping candle wax and plumping pillows, perform an abbreviated *toilette,* pay a visit to Maggion and one to the sea, and then fairly run the half-mile to the boat landing to catch the vaporetto at nine o'clock. I am going to market.

The Rialto, literally "high river," is the place, some are convinced, where the first Venetian settlement grew up. It was there that from ancient times the world's merchants came to trade and, still now, it remains the bawdy heart of Venetian commerce. The sentimental symbol of the Rialto is a peaked bridge, stretching its familiar colonnades and arches over the canal, every pilgrim's point of reference. And ploughing toward it through sunstruck summer light or the cold smoke of a February fog on the prow of a slow boat, eyes squeezed to the past, one finds old Shylock, cloaked, plumed, brooding.

I'd always found time to stroll the markets at the Rialto during past visits to Venice, thinking it charming if not quite as splendid as other of Italy's *mercati.* Now, though, it is my own, and I want to know it as an intimate. The first thing to discover is how to enter the marketplace from its backstreets rather than from the bridge and its avenue of silver and jewelry shops, kiosks hung with cheap masks and cheaper T-shirts and wagons that lure tourists with waxed apples and Chilean strawberries and cracked coconuts bathing in plastic fountains. It is further down the row that wagonsful of fruits and vegetables announce the market's genuine seductions. And hidden behind these sits the handsome edifice of the sixteenth-century tribunal of Venice.

I remembered seeing the *pretori,* judges, gowns flying, liberated from their benches for a quick coffee or a Campari, edging through heaped-up eggplants and cabbages, dodging ropes of garlic and chili peppers, to settle back again behind the solid doors of the tribunal and resume the cause of Venetian justice. Once I saw a priest and a judge, their skirts billowed up behind them, bending over a vegetable cart, Church and state, tête-à-tête, picking through the string beans. Even such folkloric scenes, though, would not draw me up and down through the bridge's daily carnival. I try debarking from the vaporetto one stop before the Rialto at San Silvestro. I walk under a tunnel and out into the *ruga,* stepping directly into the dazzle of the market.

I hear it, feel it, the shivery pull of the Casbah, another call of the wild. I walk faster, faster yet, tilting left past a cheese shop and the pasta lady, finally braking in front of a table so sumptuously laid as to be awaiting Caravaggio. I move slowly, touching when I dare, trying a smile now and then, knowing neither where nor how to begin. I walk to the *pescheria,* fish market, a clamorous hall full of the stinging, dizzying perfumes of sea salt and fish blood where every writhing, slithering, slinking, swimming, crawling, sea-breathing, jewel-eyed creature that would be hauled up from the Adriatic glitters on thick marble pallets. I look in on the *macellerie,* butchers, who are cutting nearly transparent steaks behind their macabre curtains of rabbits, wild and tame, hung from their hind legs, with tufts of fur left clinging at their haunches to serve as proof that they are not feline.

Perhaps the most Venetian of all the *botteghe* in the Rialto is Drogheria Mascari, a shop still trafficking in spices. An ounce of cloves, a fistful of *pepe di Giamaica,* allspice berries, nutmegs big as apricots, foot-long sticks of cinnamon bark with a hot-sweet perfume, black chestnut honey from the Friuli, teas, coffees, chocolates, fruits, candied or drowned in liqueurs. I longed to pull paper and coins from the small black purse hung across my chest and place the money into the merchants' rough hard hands. More horrible than it was when I had no money to buy these things, this is another sort of hunger. I want everything, but, for now, I am alone with a baroque appetite. I buy peaches, ripely blushing, small bouquets of maroon-veined white lettuces, a melon whose perfect muskiness totters on the edge of mold.

The shoppers are mostly women, housewives of all ages, all physical proportions, and a rather universal voice pitched somewhere beyond a scream. They propel *carrelli,* market carts, lined in large plastic bags, and one is convinced, fast and well, to stay clear of them. There are clusters of old men engaged in—among other things— the sober trade of arugula and dandelion greens and other bouquets of wild grasses tied up with cotton string. The farmers are sublime hucksters, rude, sweet, mocking. They are showmen taunting in slippery dialect and theirs is a whole other language for me to learn. *"Ciapa sti pomi, che xe così bei."* What's he saying? He is offering me a slice of apple? *"Tasta, tasta bea mora; i costa solo che do schei.* Taste, taste, pretty black-haired lady; they cost so little."

Not so many mornings pass before smiles are swapped, before I can ask one or another of them to bring me some mint or marjoram the next day, to save a quart of blackberries. There is Michele with a fluff of blond curls and a flushed face to set off his thick golden chains, and Luciano, architect of the Caravaggio table, and the ginger lady with her long cracked nails and the green woolen cap I would see her wear in summer and winter. They are all of a seductive society, collaborators in a crack theater troupe. One holds out a single, silky pea pod or a fat purple fig with honeyed juices trickling out from its heat-broken skin, another whacks open a small, round watermelon called *anguria* and offers a sliver of its icy red flesh from the point of a knife. To upstage the watermelon man, another cuts through the pale green skin of a cantaloupe, holding out a salmon-pink wedge of it cradled on a brown paper sack. And yet another one shouts, "The pulp of this peach is white as your skin."

⌒

One morning, while waiting for two veal chops at the *macellaio*, I hear a woman say, *"Puoi darmi un orecchio?* Can you give me an ear?" How nice, I think. She wants a conference with her butcher. Perhaps she wants him to save scraps for her cats, to procure a fat capon for next Saturday. Sebastiano descends from his sawdusted stage and his lemon-oiled wooden block, disappears into the sanctum of his cold room and returns holding up high a great rosy flounce of translucent flesh. *"Questo può andar bene, signora?* Will this be okay, ma'am?" She approves with pursed lips and half-closed eyes. Sold. One pig's ear. *"Per insaporire i fagioli.* To flavor the beans," she justifies to no one in particular.

Perhaps my favorite market visit is with the egg lady, who always sets up her table in a different position, her shiftings dependent, I come to understand, on which way the wind is blowing. She seeks to protect her hens. Hers is a fascinating act. Each morning from her farm on the island of Sant'Erasmo she transports five or six old biddies inside a cotton flour sack. Once at market, she nestles the sack of fluttering hens under her table, bends down low and begins warbling in dialect. *"Dai, dai me putei, faseme dei bei vovi.* Come on my little babies, make beautiful eggs for me." Every once in a while she opens the sack for a quick search. On her table is a pile of old newspapers torn into neat squares and a reed basket with a high-arched handle in which she places each new egg with the gentleness, one imagines, of a Bellini Madonna. On the days when she brings two, even three sacks of hens, the basket is almost always full. Other mornings see it with only a few. As they are sold, she wraps each egg in newspaper, twisting both ends so that the confection looks like a rustic prize for a child's party. If one wants six eggs, one waits while she fashions the six prizes. When the old reed basket is empty and a customer comes forward, she asks him to be patient, to wait only a moment, as she bends to her covey in whispery cheer. Damp, then, with the triumph of a midwife, she presents the warm, creamy-shelled treasures.

An ancient named Lidia brings fruit to sell. Always swaddled in layers of shawls and sweaters, an all-season costume that seemed to suffocate her spare self in summer and leave her in shivers in the winter, she has apples and pears in autumn, peaches, plums, apricots, cherries, and figs in summer, and in the interim, Lidia plies her bounty sun-dried. I loved to go to her in the thick of the Adriatic winter when, in a hugger-mugger of fogs, the market seemed a tiny kingdom in the sky. It was then that she would tend a quiet fire in an old coal scuttle, keeping it close enough to comfort her legs and feet, every once in a while roasting her hands back into circulation. Lidia buried apples deep in the heaps of smoldering ash. And just when the hot flesh sent perfumes of solace up through the mists, she'd take a long fork and pull one forth, blackened, burst, soft as pudding. Carefully peeling away its cindery crust, she would eat the pale, wine-smelling flesh with a small wood-handled spoon. One day I tell her about a lady I know in the market in Palmanova up in the Friuli. I tell her that she, too, roasts apples in her foot-warming fire, each red beauty cuddled up in a leaf of savoy cabbage. When the apples are soft, she discards the charred leaf that keeps fruit from ash and eats them between elegant nips from her rum flask. Lidia thinks this fillip with the cabbage leaf a travesty. As for the rum chaser, only the Friuliani, she says, could suffer so brutish a concoction. A rustic aesthete in a beaver vest, she asks who but they could abide the stench of burning cabbage. *"I Friuliani sono praticamente slavi, sai.* The Friuliani are practically Slavs, you know," she confides.

The hours I spent in the custody of this society linger, crystalline, as they will for all my days. They taught me about food and cooking and patience. I learned about the moon and the sea, about war and hunger and feasting. They sang me their songs and told me their stories and, over time, they became my chosen family and I their chosen child. I feel the rough touches of their gnarly hands and their wet, sour-breathed kisses; I see the rheumy color of their old eyes that changed as the sea changed. They are Venice's downstairs maids and butlers, the ones content with their portion in this life, descendants of Venetian women who never wove pearls in their hair, descendants of Venetian men who never wore satin breeches or sipped China tea at Florian. These are the other Venetians, the ones who rode the lagoons from their island farms to market, day after day, stopping only to fish for supper or to say prayers in some country church, never even once having walked in Piazza San Marco.

As I passed by Michele's table one day, his head was bent into the work of weaving the dried stems of small silver onions into braids. Without looking up at me he freed his hands to hold out a branch of tomatoes, each one so small it looked like a tight rosebud. I pulled at one and rolled it around in my mouth, chewed it slowly. Its savor and perfume were that of a two-pound sun-warmed tomato distilled, suspended inside the tiny ruby fruit. Still with his head bent, Michele asked, *"Hai capito?* Have you understood?" Short for "Have you understood that these are the earth's most beautiful tomatoes?" He knew very well I'd understood.

And as if the market were not gift enough, Cantina do Mori was tucked nearby in a quiet *ruga* just off the market's center. I loved to stay inside the narrow lantern-lit room to watch the droll march that began much earlier in the morning than I would ever see. The reprises were endless, though: Plastic-aproned fishmongers, butchers in bloodied smocks, lettuce farmers and orchard workers, almost every man in the market pageant would, at approximate half-hour intervals, step through the door and sidle up to its fifteenth-century bar as merchants and gentlemen and brigands had been doing for more than half a thousand years before them. Then, with certain subtle movements of head, eyes, fingers, each calls for his cup. They gulp the Prosecco, the Refosco, the Incrocio Manzoni in a single swallow, two perhaps if they are speaking at the same time, slam down the emptied glass and the proper coinage, and walk out the backdoor to work. Often I was the only woman there besides the tourists or a rare visit from a female shopkeeper, but all of us were tended to by a gentle moon raker called Roberto Biscotin. He has been cooking and pouring and smiling his Jimmy Stewart smile there for forty years. And there are always very separate acts being played on his stage.

Japanese tourists call for Sassacaia at thirty thousand lire a glass, Germans drink beer, Americans read aloud from their guidebooks, the English are distressed there are no chairs or tables, the French never like the wine, and the Australians always seem tipsy. And all of them are wallpaper to the locals.

At noon or so the market quiets, shoppers start for home, and workers pay attention to their appetites. Roberto is ready with truffled *panini, tramezzini* of roasted ham or smoked trout, chunks of whiffy cheese, great platters of artichokes, tiny pickled onions wrapped in anchovy, and barrels and bottles of local and not-so-local wines.

During my first winter, after my loyalty had been noted for a few months running, Roberto would offer to take my coat, my string bag full of market stuffs and put everything back in the kitchen so I could be freer. I would eat and drink according to the weather and he state of my hungers, and I remember my stand-up meals there as among the most satisfying of my life. Slowly I began to know the other faithfuls, to engage in the badinage that stitched one day to the next—who'd had a fever, who had gallstones, the state of repairs on Roberto's Harley, the way to stew fresh fava beans in the fireplace, where to find a secret porcini cache in the Treviso forests, why I'd come to live in Italy, why it is an Italian man's destiny to be unfaithful. The sheepishness they first felt because of me eases, but slowly. When they begin to surrender formal addresses for winey three-kiss hugs and *"Ci vediamo domani.* We'll see you tomorrow," I know I have yet another room in my house.

They speak nearly exclusively in dialect, and I nearly exclusively in Italian during those first months—that is, when I wasn't falling back into English or that Esperanto thing. Inside Do Mori, my social circle is composed of a butcher and a fishmonger, a cheeseman, an artichoke farmer, a local landscape artist, a portrait photographer, a few retired railway workers, two shoemakers, and a couple of dozen others to whom I am connected, for an hour or so each day, by sympathy. We gather there because it is a place where others would notice, regret even, should one of us not be there. The market and its little cantina are my refuge from that still-hovering malaise, a balm against the quiet grief that comes, once in a while, with big doles of unmarked time in a city that's not yet home.

Do Mori closes for a few hours at one-thirty in the afternoon and, mostly, I am the last to leave. I don't like pushing through the swinging doors, stepping out into the soundlessness of the *ruga*. Tables stripped, pavements swept of carrot tops, fishmarket floor washed clean, glistening, the hush is checked only by a few snarls from resident cats in battle over a butcher's gift and the click, clicking of my heels as I walk away. Now begins of the second part of my day.

Only the trattorias and restaurants are open, and everyone not lunching out is at home, at table or in bed until at least four. Often my appetite is satisfied by Roberto's antipasti, and I don't stop in somewhere else to sit for a proper lunch. What I desire is to drift in some far-flung quarter.

Perhaps no one ever gets to know Venice as much as they remember her, recall her from an episode in some other dream. Venice is all our fantasies. Water, light, color, perfume, escape, disguise, license are gold spun and stitched into the skirts she trails across her stones by day and spreads out over her lagoon in the never-quite-blackness of her nights. I followed where Venice led me. I learn which benches stay shady, where waits the most potent espresso ice, when the afternoon bake is ready at which *panificio,* which churches are always open, and which bells can be pulled to summon a shuffling sacristan from his *pisolino,* nap. One, his great iron keys threaded on a length of green ribbon, leads me with a candle to see a Jacopo Bellini that floats from frayed amber cords in the chiaroscuro of a tiny back room in his church. The old man's eyes are unpolished sapphires, and, in the haze of a thousand years of incense burned, he tells me tales of Canaletto, of Guardi and Titian and Tiepolo. He speaks of them as though they are his confidants, the fellows with whom he sups on Thursday nights. He says life is a search for beauty and that art dissolves loneliness. His and mine, I think. I am not alone. I am a wanderer in a blue felt cloche, come to Venice to stitch together her fantasies.

━

But I know myself, and stitching fantasies just won't be enough to keep me upright. I need to cook my heart out. And if I can't cook for our own table, I'll cook for someone else's table. But whose? I think of the troll and her posse. No. I decide on the inmates at the bank. A white chocolate and raspberry tart one day; on another day, one made with tiny yellow plums called *susine*. I risk bread, still warm and fat with whole hazelnuts, its own pot of brandied mascarpone as accessory. These I tuck in a basket and leave at the front desk like foundlings. There are eleven who work there with Fernando, one or other of whom is forever ordering up trays of pastries and cups of gelato and bottles of Prosecco to be carted over from Pasticceria Rosasalva, so I think the dainties will please. Rather they confound, impose upon them, and before Fernando has to ask, I discontinue the Red Riding Hood visits and go back to my stitching.

One evening Fernando and I have supper at a place in the Ruga Rialto, a bawdy workingmen's *osteria,* just taken over by a man called Ruggero. A rambling type, a newcomer to Venice, he thought to dazzle the simple folk by bringing them back a piece of their own gastronomic history. Ruggero is a showman who works his house like a stage. He pounds a ship's gong whenever the cook brings forth some great bowl of watery risotto or pasta washed in squid ink and plunks it down on the bar. Ruggero then portions it out to his customers for a modest four thousand lire a head. There are whole wheels of creamy mountain cheeses and rounds of crusty bread from the baker round the corner, a white fluff of pounded salt cod and a tub of boiled beans dressed with olive oil and sweet onions. These, with the essential sardines lolling in puckery sauce, are his menu. Cold, white wine flows fast from the spigot into one's tumbler and, midst the noises of a hundred hungry, thirsty Venetians, one stands or sits at rough, acid-green paper-covered tables and sups in the way of the once-upon-a-time *bacari,* the wine bars. Fernando and I love the spectacle.

"The people from the market tell me you're a chef," says Ruggero to me one evening. "Why don't you cook here one night and we'll have a party. We'll invite some people from the neighborhood, merchants and judges and such. You write the menu, I'll do the shopping, you cook, and I'll serve," he says, all in a single breath. Fernando is kicking me hard under the table, clearly wanting nothing to do with this Ruggero fellow or his private parties. But nearly each time I go to the Rialto, I seem to run into Ruggero. Each time he talks about the party. When he involves my market friends Michele and Roberto I say "yes," not waiting for blessings from the stranger.

I want to cook regional American food for Venetians. I think it will be great fun for them, thinking as they do that all Americans, *poverini,* poor little things, subsist, barely, on microwaved, barbecue-flavored popcorn. I plan a six-course dinner for fifty guests. I ask Ruggero to show me the kitchen. Caverns, holes, magnificently appointed, appointed not at all, I've worked in all of them, and no behind-the-swinging-doors tableau can frighten me. Ruggero's kitchen frightens me. The same ancient fat that fouls the kitchen's air also paves its floors. The gas oven is rusted and its door hangs open from a broken hinge. The few tools and equipment are neolithic. The water runs only on cold. I think back to all the suppers I have eaten that were made in this mire while he is telling me that most of his food is prepared at another restaurant and carted over to him each day, that the only dishes his cook prepares in-house are the *primi*—risotto, minestrone pasta. I try furiously to remember if I ever ate one such dish but I can't think for the nausea.

Have the powers of the Italian state sanctioned this kitchen? I look for his license, and there it is all stamped and sealed and under glass up on the greasy wall. I still haven't said a word when he begins to tell me that he'll have the place *bello ordinato,* in good order, for me next week. He shows me a box of cleaning supplies acquired in my honor. He says a friend is coming to work on the oven, that a plumber is, in fact, due tomorrow morning. He says all we really need are enthusiasm and fresh ideas, a good spirit, and we'll have a fine party.

Ruggero's cook is a woman in her fifties with shoe-black hair and red tights, and now, when Ruggero goes to take a telephone call, she asks if I know Donato, and I say I don't think so. She says he's the *capitano della guardia di finanza,* the captain of the tax-control force, who comes to lunch each day and often to dinner each evening and that it is he who "arranged" for Ruggero's license. She opens the door and nods toward Donato and his lunch. I really want this experience of cooking American food for Venetians, but I tell Ruggero that until he makes a little progress in the kitchen, I can't promise. It's Tuesday, and he tells me to come Thursday evening for supper and to have another look.

Fernando can't imagine why I want to eat first at La Vedova even though we are going to Ruggero's. I tell him to trust me for once and he does. We walk over to Ruggero's and head straight back into the kitchen. I have said almost nothing to prepare Fernando, and it's a good thing because he would have told me how I exaggerated. The old place sparkles as much as it could. Pine and ammonia have rescued the air, new rubber mats are laid on the cleaner floors, shiny aluminum pots and other modest *batterie* hang overhead. The cook is wearing a white apron. Before Ruggero has a chance to join us, she tells us that he offered a group of regular customers a free lunch and all the wine they could drink in exchange for two hours of work cleaning the kitchen. She says half a dozen of them worked, and then another crew replaced them, and another, and that this is the result. She says the oven is hopeless and the plumber never showed, but isn't the rest just wonderful? Still wary, I nevertheless sit with Ruggero to write the menu.

There will be Mississippi caviar—even though I'll have to substitute *borlotti* beans for black-eyed peas—and skillet cornbread, oyster stew, soft-shelled crabs in browned butter, pan-roasted pepper-crusted beef in Kentucky bourbon sauce with potato pancakes and batter-fried onions, hot fudge pudding with brown-sugared cream. Ruggero is surprised at the shopping list, which seems shy of exotic "American" components, and I tell him it's what we'll do with the oysters and the soft-shelled crabs and the beef and the chocolate that will translate them into American dishes. I ask him to please keep the kitchen clean and to do the shopping, that I'm off to Tuscany for a few days. I don't mention the oven or the plumber.

News of the party travels through the Rialto, and when I go to

market on the morning before, everyone wants to talk about it. It is
a thing sweet to me that these people, who take for granted their
gold-lit lives in the water kingdom, can be so curious about deep-
fried onion rings and how whisky tastes with beefsteak. Fernando
and Ruggero are my sous-chefs, and our only difficulties seem to be
keeping would-be helpers out of our way. Neither the oven nor the
water gets hot, but we cook and fry and sauté and serve and eat and
drink. I take my anadama breads to bake in the *panificio* down the al-
ley, trading a few loaves for oven rent. Ruggero, the showman, wears
a tuxedo. Ruggero, the impresario, has engaged two classical guitar
students from the conservatory Benedetto Marcello, and they play
Fernando Sor in the candlelight between the two long tables in the
strange little room behind the bar on the alleyway near the marketplace across the canal from the Rialto Bridge in Venice. Each of
these facts excites me.

After everything is done, I take a dish of pudding and sit
down between my fishmonger and Roberto and I notice Donato, the captain of the tax-control force with the good appetite,
conferencing with the guitarists and nodding my way. Ruggero
asks for attention and the room quiets. A slow, taunting *Gelosia,*
Jealousy, is throbbing out from the guitars and, without so much
as asking, Donato is kissing my hand, leading me, flushed from
the burners and with chocolate on my breath, to tango between
the tables. Thank goodness for those lessons Misha gave me as a
present so many years ago. All those Tuesday nights with Señora
Carmela and the clammy-palmed computer prodigies from IBM.
The languid glide, the abrupt, explosive half-twist. ("Restraint,
restraint my loves," warned Señora Carmela. "Black arched, neck

elongated, chin up, higher, higher, eyes direct, unblinking, smoldering," she'd say in an almost menacing whisper.) I've never
tangoed anywhere but in the Poughkeepsie middle school gym.
Now I am gliding and half-twisting in the arms of a picaresque
official of the state who is moving beautifully in tight, gray uni-
form pants. I should be dressed in something smooth and red,
my hair should smell of roses rather than fried onions, and I
don't think I'm smoldering nearly enough. Donato is smoldering
somewhat more than enough though, and Venetians are on their
feet, cheering. Fernando senses it's time to go.

While the guests slide deeper into their cups, we say a quiet
good-night to Ruggero and head for the beach. We go out through
the bar and see that a group of old men, their backs to us, are hud-
dled around the huge bowl that held the hot fudge pudding, scraping at what is left with teaspoons, licking their fingers clean just like
all-American boys. We hear one of them say, *"Ma l'ha fatto l'americana?*
*Davvero? Ma come si chiama questo dolce?* Did the American really
make this? But what's the name of this dessert?"

# 10

# I Knew a Woman, I Knew a Man

ut there can't be a party every day. One morning I lay facedown on the fancy ocher-draped bed under the lace *baldacchino,* weeping. What is the matter with me? Fernando says it's low blood pressure. He thinks my seeing a doctor is self-indulgent, but I search the directory anyway. I learn that professional listings are not culled under specific headings. One must know the name of the doctor in order to find his or her number. I'm lost. I stop by the tourist office, and the folks there assure me that the only English-speaking doctor in Venice is an allergist. They tell me he's *simpatico.* I take their word for it and set off for his office in San Maurizio. Small, weary, chain-smoking, he interviews me from the velvety charcoal depths of a Napoleonic-era chaise longue that is positioned far across the cavernous room from my straight-backed wooden chair.

He asks, "Do you have a normal sex life?" I am perplexed. Is he suggesting I have an allergy to sex?

"I think it's normal. For me, that is," I tell him.

After a pause to converse with his housekeeper over the composition of his lunch, he stands nearby, fingers pressed to my pulse, and says, "E-e-et is only that you are scarry, *cara mia.*" I hope he means, "It is only that you are scared, my dear." I ask his fee, and he looks shocked that I would sully this tête-à-tête by speaking of money. Months later, there arrives his bill for 350,000 lire, about 175 dollars, a very special fee reserved for rich American ladies.

As I walk through the city, I begin to notice American travelers. They seem better looking than all the others, the nasaly timbre of their voices almost Pavlovian for me. As though all of them are dear friends, none of whom quite recognize me there in my Venetian surroundings, I am eager to speak to them. I sit in a café or stand on line at a gallery entrance, sleuthing for some way to engage them. Some one of them almost always gets around to asking how long I've been in Venice, or where I am going next, naturally thinking I am a traveler, too. When I tell them that I live here, that I will soon be married to an Italian, the swapping of compatriotic sympathies shifts. A wealthy friend once told me that as soon as a person discovers how much she's worth, that person's attitude toward her changes, categorizing her first as "portfolio" and second as "woman." When I tell my story, I am shuffled from the category of an American into that of an exotic and certainly I am no longer one of them. I've gone to the other side. I am good for supper recommendations, the name of a *farmacista* who'll hand out antibiotics without a prescription, or maybe an extra room for a guest in my house.

I consider joining the ranks of the British Women's Club of Venice. Perhaps they could soothe the malaise. I learn they are eighty sisters bound by a collective disenchantment with life in Italy, life with their Italian husbands. Most live on *terraferma,* the mainland, as far away as Udine and Pordenone and, hence, must trek in over the waters for this monthly commingling of Englishness. Many of them came to Italy as girls, sojourning for a summer among the dark-eyed boys, perhaps spending a year at university in Rome or Florence or Bologna, each having been a huntress on the scent of her own quarry. On the Lido I find only three.

Always wearing a turban and ropes of fake pearls, an eighty-two year old named Emma had married a Venetian city guide twelve years her junior, who soon forsook her to run off with a former paramour. Though her story is half a century old, she speaks of it like a fresh wound. Caroline, a fiftyish blond with a wonderful half-inch gap between her front teeth, rushed about her corner of the island, from baker to butcher as though bandits waited beyond the milk shop. A victim of the torpors, I think she was. I can't remember the name of the tall, sallow woman, hair shorn rather than cut, who lived near the church in San Nicolò. I was in the entryway of her home once and saw her wedding photo, the strange sweet pose of a gangly, freckled girl and a round-faced boy whose wavy pompadour barely brushed up to his bride's chin. Each time I would meet them walking about the Lido I would recall the photo and smile. I think they were still in love.

The group's president is also the wife of the British consul. She is a *siciliana* who croaks out her English in a hoarse Transylvanian accent. By the time I arrive, her husband, a small dull chap, has already been advised that the funding needed to keep the consulate plushly housed on the *piano nobile,* first floor, of a sixteenth-century palazzo across the *calle* from the Accademia is soon to end. For now though, up its grand marble staircase, inside its mahoganied seclusion, the sisterhood still gathers to tipple and munch and stir up tribal rancors. Though I find some of them charming, their familiarity with one another will be hard to penetrate. Besides, I am not so certain that twenty years from now I would like to be among them, fretting over Italy's capricious supply of gingerstem biscuits.

⌒

Each afternoon at five-thirty, I meet Fernando at the bank. I like having this rendezvous, even though his humor is almost always cranky at this hour. One evening, he tells me he needs five minutes to arrange some papers and asks me to wait in his office. He closes the door after him, and so I sit there in the big, fancy room he dislikes so because of its isolation from all the action. Its walls frescoed with coquettish nymphs, its green marble fireplace, a photo of us in Saint Louis, the scents of old leather and cigarettes and my husband's cologne, I like it here. Riffling through a financial journal, I think how very much I like it here, and I step out of my brown tulle collottes. Using a chair to boost me, I drape the pretty things over the telecamera. I sit there, then, on his desk, legs swinging out from my thin silk dress, and I wait, the marble of his desktop cold under my thighs.

Leaving the bank, we walk to the boat station. Now that we are dining more at home, Fernando begs off our after-work strolls, wanting the apartment's comfort. His feet hurt, his eyes burn, he hates the heat or the cold or the wind or whatever else the skies might be offering, he rips open his third package of cigarettes, and I fall in love again, happy that another day's wars are ended for him. He has begun to resent the bank or, more, his own noble sort of devotion to it. Safe in its communist embrace, its dependents can work or not work and still pocket the same spoils at month's end. He

wishes to sit all day among his Aperol-breathed cohorts but his
conscience rubs. Apart from a threadbare *contessa* or two whose ac-
counts he has tended for quarter of a century, his clients are mostly
hand-to-mouth merchants in the neighborhood. He frets over them,
pushes back due dates, and adjusts regulations to keep wolves in
fedoras and cashmere coats from their doors. He cares deeply about
these people, but not much about the institution of the bank itself.
He says that since our life began, his work leaves him bloodless. He
says he wants to restore furniture and learn to play the piano, to live
in the countryside somewhere, to have a garden. He says he's beginning to remember his dreams. Lord. Like a blueberry-eyed bear
feeling new muscles and rubbing his eyes at the spring light, Fernando is plotting his own *risorgimento*.

On the *motonave* back across the water, we sit always on the top
deck, never minding the weather nor how empty or how peopled
it might be in any other part of the boat. Wearing a vacant Chauncey
Gardner smile, he looks mostly out to the water, turning to me once
or twice as though to make certain I am still present. He may recount some buffoonery enacted by a colleague or, more often, his
directors. In a poignant gesture, he lifts up of a hank of my hair and
kisses it.

This evening on the boat he greets an old man, introduces him to
me as Signore Massimiliano. The man has laughing silvery eyes, and he
holds my hand in his two hands and looks at me for a long time before
he walks slowly to the exit. Fernando tells me the man was a friend of
his father's and that, when he was a boy, Massimiliano used to take him
fishing along the Riva Sette Martiri for *passarini,* tiny fish Venetians
like to fry and eat, bones and all. He says that when he was about ten or

eleven and spending a lot of time playing billiards in the Castello rather than going to school, Massimiliano sat with him one day and asked him if he'd prefer to marry a girl who liked boys who shoot pool or boys who read Dante. Fernando says he asked him why he couldn't marry a girl who liked boys who shoot pool and who also read Dante and the man told him it wasn't possible, so he said he'd prefer the girl who liked boys who read Dante, of course. Massimiliano looked at him and asked, "Don't you think you'd better be getting ready for her?" Fernando says the man's words hit him like rocks, that he read Dante day in and day out, waiting for this girl to come along. He says how strange it is, sometimes, which conversation or event stays with us while so much else melts fast as April snow. Yes, I tell him.

I say I knew a woman who went to see *Man of la Mancha* on Broadway and then walked from the theater down to Chelsea, back uptown to her apartment, and packed everything she wanted from her life there while her husband slept. "She told me she climbed into bed and she slept, too, for a few hours and later, from the airport, she called her boss to say good-bye. She went to Paris that morning to think, and she's still in Paris, thinking. But she's fine, she's better," I tell him.

He says, "I knew a man who told me he'd betrayed his wife throughout their long marriage because the Madonna appeared to him on the night before his wedding and absolved him of all future guilt. For forty years he went peacefully into the night to prowl. He said the same dispensation was valid for his sons." It is my turn.

I tell him, "I knew a woman who was being crushed by her husband's philandering, and when her doctor told her if she didn't leave him she would die, she asked him, *'But what about all that history? We've been together for almost thirty years.'* The doctor asked her, 'And so you're aiming at thirty-one? You will sustain your rage, using time as a defense against fear and indolence. In the great stash of defenses, time is the one least imaginative,' he told her." His turn.

"I knew a man who said, 'Some people ripen, some rot. We grow, sometimes, but we never change. Can't do it. No one can. Who we are is fixed. There isn't a soul who can unfix another soul, not even his own,' he said."

I tell him, "I knew a man who sat with his freshly estranged wife outdoors at the Saloon near Lincoln Center and, over fried zucchini, he asked her if she'd loved him, and she said, 'I can't remember. Perhaps I did, but I just can't remember.'" He looks at me hard and shoots my own words back at me.

"I know a woman who says it's only at three o'clock in the morning when anyone can measure things. She says if you love yourself at three o'clock in the morning, if there's someone in your bed that you love at least as much as you love yourself at three o'clock in the morning, if your heart is quiet in your chest and neither muses nor shades crowd the room, it probably means things are well. It's the hardest moment to lie to yourself, three o'clock in the morning, she told me."

We play "I knew a woman, I knew a man" most nights coming home on the boat, and the game seems to ease away the banker and bring forth Fernando. Back at home, refreshed by our bath, his martini, his Prufrock supper, he remembers how to laugh.

⌒

One autumn Saturday morning Fernando chides my use of the familiar form *tu* in addressing a gentleman to whom he introduces me as we stand on the deck of a vaporetto. The man is about sixty-five, handsome, suave in his foulard and silk suit. A flicker of strain, something sharp passes between them. Had I blundered so badly? As we walk through Venice Fernando grows silent, surly even. I am perplexed that a *tu* rather than a *Lei* could grieve him so. This almighty *bella figura* thing? Finally we sit inside at Florian, and he begins to speak. He tells me the story of the man on the vaporetto. He is a doctor who has kept offices on the Lido for as long as Fernando can remember. He says his mother had been the doctor's mistress. It was an alliance that splattered out over and smothered a dozen years of his childhood. He says it was as though someone else—someone more important than his father or his brother Ugo or himself—lived in their house. Never discussed, this unnamed tyranny destroyed them. There was no mercy from the Lidensi. Vicious and tormenting, they proclaimed the scandal the great cuckolding of its time. His father withdrew to one part of the house, entered into a protracted illness, and took years and years to die of heart problems, both organic and sentimental.

"You still grieve for him," I say.

"Not *still*," he says quickly. "I grieve for him because now I *can*, unfrozen, unlocked by the lady in the long white coat. I'm content we saw Onofrio, and I'm more content you gave him the *tu*. But I'm sorry for my father. I'm sorry he went into his long, dark night "a man," a silent, suffering *bella figura*. He left me with the torch. It was my turn to become quiet and choked and brave and without needs of my own. I was to be the next generation, the next virtuous bearer of old miseries. I won't do it, I won't be another man like my father, stepping over the cracks, lurking about the spaces of his own life like a visitor, fearing more to disturb, to offend, to be *too present* than he feared to die."

As long as that dying was, he said, his brother's death in the same year happened in an instant.

Having long ago fled the Lido and his counterfeit family, Ugo had been a diplomat in the service of the European Parliament in Luxembourg. He was forty when he died from a heart attack. "The echoes feel like bricks on my chest," Fernando says. Ugo and I spoke only once about the affair, one night when he was fifteen and I was twelve. We were alone in our room, lying in our beds in the dark and smoking. I asked him if it was true, and all he said was yes. Until now, I've never spoken to anyone else about it."

"Tell me about Ugo," I say. "What was he like?"

"He was like you. Irrepressible, enchanted by things, he lived on the edges of his moments. He could fit a whole life inside an hour. Everything that happened to him was an adventure. I would go down to the ferry to meet him whenever he came back for a few days. He drove a two-seater Morgan with the top down even in winter, and he wore a long white scarf. He kept Champagne in the boot and a red felt case with two Baccarat flutes. The day we met and you pulled out that goblet from its little velvet pouch and your silver flask of cognac, my heart turned over."

We didn't say anything for a long time until he raised up his head and looked at me hard. There was no stranger in his gaze. There was only Fernando.

# Ah, Cara Mia, in Six Months Everything Can Change in Italy

*L*iving as a couple never means that each gets half. You must take turns at giving more than getting. It's not the same as a bow to the other whether to dine out rather than in, or which one gets massaged that evening with oil of calendula; there are seasons in the life of a couple that function, I think, a little like a night watch. One stands guard, often for a long time, providing the serenity in which the other can work at something. Usually that something is sinewy and full of spines. One goes inside the dark place while the other one stays outside, holding up the moon. I know I must not lean on Fernando right now. Reckonings, hungers, irregular verbs, these are mine alone to fathom while he uses his energy to come clean with himself, to do his own *weeding and scrubbing and digging clear down to China*. He has work to do, so I'll provide the peace. As much as I want him to love me, I want Fernando to love himself.

I think he also wants to love himself. He is not only awakening, he has taken up the cudgels. "In order to breathe, he must break all the windows," said Virginia Woolf about James Joyce. I try to imagine what she would say of Fernando. I say he's a Mamluk with reins

between his teeth, wielding twin scimitars, robes flying, gold jan-
gling, riding like hell across hot sands into the French phalanx.

"Let's tear down the walls," he says figuratively one morning, "all
of them, and while we're at it, let's smash in the doors." I think he
is saying, I want to breathe. "New bathroom, hah. New furniture,
hah. Everything that ever happened before was surreal," he says.
"I've had a sort of hand-me-down life that never fit, that was never
my own. Now I feel like a Jew ready to walk out of Egypt," he says
quietly.

Lord! Why is he always so heavy?

"Can you keep up with me?" he wants to know, sparklers lighting up his eyes. "For example, did you know that we're getting married on October 22?" It is now early September.

"Of what year?" I want to know.

We had begun the hesitation waltz with the Ufficio Stato Civile
on the Lido six weeks earlier. Loins girded, hearts stout, we would
accommodate the state's gluttony for declarations and submissions
and disclosures; we would fill the works with signatures and testimonies and stamps and seals. We would have our license to be
married. On the first Saturday morning visit, as we climb the stone
stairs up to the tiny city hall next to the carabinieri barracks, I believe I am a pilgrim fit to travel through the prickly wilderness of the
Italian bureaucracy. Armed in patience and calm, shielded by my
portfolio full of papers stamped by the *palermitana* in Saint Louis,
*viciously, repeatedly, with the great inked seal of the Italian state,* I am near
to the finish. Only details remain, it will be a piece of cake, I think,
as we stand in line to see the secretary. Fernando tells me to smile

rather than try to talk. He says the bureaucracy is always more indulgent to the helpless, and so I am meek as Teresa the Little Flower. The secretary tells us that *la direttrice* is, of course, occupied and asks why we hadn't fixed an appointment. Fernando assures her that he has called, left telephone messages and two hand-delivered written messages beseeching *la direttrice.*

*"Ah, certo, siete voi. Lei è l'americana.* Ah, yes, it's you. You're the American," says the secretary, looking me up and down. She wears white jeans, a U-2 T-shirt, and forty bangle bracelets and carries a pack of Dunhill's and matches in case she needs to light up during the twelve-yard voyages she makes from her office to *la direttrice's* office. We sit and wait, grinning at each other. "Here we are," we say, "getting things under way."

From nine-thirty until nearly noon the Little Flower and the stranger wait, he breaking the vigil at half-hour intervals with an espresso from the bar down on Sandro Gallo. Once he brings back espresso for me, china cup and saucer and spoon, an almond croissant all on a small tray. *"Simpatico,"* the secretary says of Fernando, before she tells us to come back next Saturday.

The next Saturday and the Saturday after that pass in much the same way, modified only by our taking turns to go to the bar. Four Saturdays pass without our seeing *la direttrice.* This is an island of seventeen thousand citizens, sixteen thousand of whom are on the beach every Saturday in summer while the rest are at home watching *Dallas* reruns. Who can be in there with her? On the fifth Saturday, the Little Flower and the stranger are shown directly into her office. *La direttrice* is gray. She is all gray. Her skin, her lips, her hair, her baggy linen dress are all the color of ashes. She exhales a gray cloud, extinquishes her cigarette, and holds out her large gray hand in welcome, I think, but, in fact, to take my portfolio. She turns each page as though my documents repel her, as though they are blueprints soaked in hell broth. She smokes. Fernando smokes. The secretary comes in to file a sheaf of papers, and she smokes. I sit there trying to distract myself by looking at the print of the sacred heart of Jesus. I say "Jesus," and wonder how long it will take for me, a pink-lunged woman who has chased and captured free radicals and religiously swallowed antioxidants for ten years, to die of second-hand smoke. The *direttrice*'s glasses fall repeatedly from the end of her nose, so she picks up Fernando's, which he has laid casually on her desk, but these do not appear to help.

She closes the portfolio and says, "These papers are old and without value. The laws have changed." The Little Flower gives forth a short shriek.

"Old? These were prepared in March, and it is August," I tell her.

"Ah, *cara mia,* in six months everything can change in Italy. We are a country in movement. The government changes, the soccer coaches change, everything changes as much as nothing changes, and you must learn this, *cara mia.* You must return to America, establish residency, wait one year and refile your documents," she says without condolence. The Little Flower wilts, fights a faint.

From beyond my swoonings I hear Fernando saying *"Ma è un vero peccato perchè lei è giornalista.* It's really a shame because she is a journalist." He tells her I write for a group of very important newspapers in America, that they have assigned me to chronicle my new life here in Italy and to write a series of articles about my experiences, about the personalities who help me to find my way. Especially, he tells her, the editors are interested in the story of her marriage. She has deadlines, signora, deadlines. These articles will be read by millions of Americans and those personalities about whom she writes are bound for celebrity in the States. *La direttrice* removes Fernando's glasses and puts back her own. She does this exchange several times while I look at Fernando with a mixture of awe and disgust. He has lied through his long white teeth.

"You know I would like nothing better than to help you," she says really looking at us for the first time. I do *not* know that, I think. Now, pressing hands to temples she says. "I must go to the mayor, to the regional administrators. Could you write here the names of these very important newspapers?"

"I will write everything for you, signora, and deliver it on Monday morning," he promises. She tells us to return next Saturday, then we shall see. I begin to understand that it is not so much that the Italian bureauacracy is, itself, twisted, as it is twisted by those who administer it, who inlay and torture it, with their own set of corruptions, personal as thumbprints. There is fundamentally no Italian bureaucracy, only Italian bureaucrats. Fernando decides to tell *la direttrice* the Associated Press itself has assigned me this series of articles, and hence it is possible that hundreds, thousands of newspapers across America will pick up the stories. He writes all this in a telegram. I think it is diabolical. I pray it works. *La direttrice* telegrams in response. The troll delivers it, the easy-to-open, resealable envelope still warm from her manipulations.

"*Tutto fattibile entro tre settimane. Venite sabato mattina.* All is possible within three weeks. Come on Saturday morning."

"What do we do when she asks to see the articles?" I want to know.

"We'll tell her that America is a country in movement, that assignments change, that everything changes as much as nothing changes, and that she must understand this, *cara mia.*"

The state feels good in our pockets, but the indulgence of Mother Church remains suspended. We had learned from a single terse audience at the Curia in Venice that the sanction of the church can only be gained—if it is to be gained at all—through a mysterious investigation "that satisfies the bishop of the couple's avowed intentions to live within the church's laws." The searching of Fernando's spiritual past would be easy, but why did they need to minister the Inquisition on my behalf? Did they want the names and addresses of my churches and priests in New York and Sacramento and Saint Louis? Did they have some great papal Internet where all they had to do was punch up my name and check on my every spiritual peccadillo? And I hope these "avowed intentions to live within the church's laws" did not include birth control directives. Even if I had only hours of fertility left, I wanted no one to tell me what to do with them. I am broken by too many laws, old laws, new laws.

"We have permission from the state, the city hall is beautiful, let's just get married there," I say.

The stranger says no. Though he has tiptoed about behind the last pew of the church all his adult life, now he wants ritual, incense, candlelight, benedictions, altar boys, white carpets, and orange blossoms. He wants high mass in the red stone church that looks to the lagoon.

On a suffocating July evening we sit in the sacristy waiting for Don Silvano, the curate of Santa Maria Elisabetta. Once we get through the social groundings and chatter, the priest says something about how nice it will be to have us "young people" as communicants. I can only wonder at the average age of his congregation. We must attend classes every Tuesday evening, along with other prospective couples, to be instructed in the "moral imperatives inherent in a Roman Church–sanctioned marriage." Lord! What about our own moral imperatives? Why does he make it sound as though we would have none without his telling us we must? He has the sweet round face of a country preacher and punctuates each phrase with *benone,* great good, but still he speaks in sermons.

We had begun our instruction classes late in July. One Tuesday when we arrive, the priest takes us aside, tells us our papers are not sufficient, that the Curia has denied us permission to be married in the church. What is lacking, we want to know. "Well, for one thing," he says to me, "your certificate of confirmation is still missing."

"I don't know that I've ever seen my certificate of confirmation. I don't even know if I was ever confirmed a soldier of Christ," I tell the priest. We go to walk along the sea, and Fernando says it was a grave mistake to admit I was unsure of having been confirmed. I should only offer information necessary for their search and simply let them keep working at it. "But it's probably a wild-goose chase. Isn't it better to just receive the sacrament of confirmation now?" We go back to Don Silvano with the idea, and after he says *benone* two or three times, he tells us that I'll have to join the next confirmation class, which will begin its studies at the end of September, and, if all goes well, I can walk down the aisle with a group of ten year olds to receive the sacrament in April. April? On the way home I ask again why we can't be happy with a civil marriage. Fernando just smiles.

⌒

So on this morning in September, when the stranger announces we'll be married in October, I am wordless as stone. Is he forgetting it took six weeks just to get through the state's papers. The church could take months. Years.

When I find my voice I want to know, "Are you going to use the Associated Press story on Don Silvano?

"Not at all. I have an idea much better suited to him," he says.

Fernando tells Don Silvano he wants to be married on October 22 because that was the day in 1630 when la Serenissima sent out the decree that a great basilica would be built along the Grand Canal, dedicated to the Virgin Mother in thanks for her deliverence of Venice from the plague. Santa Maria della Salute, it was to be named. Saint Mary of Health. He has pulled at the old priest's heartstrings. *"Che bell'idea,"* he says. "Such sympathy is rare. That a man desires to combine his sacred marriage with the sacred history of Venice is something the Curia must consider. And besides, the certificate of confirmation is bound to appear sooner or later. I will offer my personal testimony to the bishop. Are you certain you don't want the ceremony to be on November 21, on the festival of la Salute?" he asks.

"No. I want October 22 because it was when the whole idea was initiated. It was the beginning. This is about beginnings, Father," says the stranger.

"October 22 it will be," says the priest.

"You just lied to a priest," I tell him, as he pulls me across the avenue and onto the vaporetto. He lets out a long loud whoop, and I realize, this is the first time I've ever heard the stranger scream.

"I did not lie! I do want us to be married on that day, which is indeed the day when the government gave Longhena the go-ahead to begin construction on la Salute. It's all true, and I'll show it to you later in black and white in Lorenzetti. And besides, Don Silvano was waiting for me to insist, he was waiting for me to give him something with which he could battle the bishop on our behalf. I had to choose a day and be aggressive about it or else nothing would happen for ages. I understand how things work and don't work here. *Furbizia innocente,* innocent cunning, is all it takes to live in Italy," he tells me. "The church, the state, and everyone in between can be compelled by the smallest stab at ego or sentiment. In the end we Italians are Candide more than we are Machiavelli. For all our historical reputation as fabulists and libertines, we are more often soft-touch emotional bunglers always looking about to be admired. We hope to keep duping the world and even each other, but we know who we are. And now let's just be quiet and revel in the fact that we have a wedding date," says the stranger.

He takes me to La Vedova behind Cà d'Oro for supper and Ada, whom I've known since my first trip to Venice, makes hand-rolled whole-wheat pasta in duck sauce and liver with onions. We drink an Amarone from Le Ragosa, and we never stop smiling. When Ada sends round the word that we're getting married in October, every shopkeeper and local who comes through the door insists on another *brindisi,* a toast. No one understands when we drink to the health of *la grigia* and *il prete,* the gray one and the priest.

One evening we pack our supper basket and drive down to the *murazzi,* the great wall of rocks planted by the Lidensi in the six-teenth century to shield the little island from the tempests of the sea. I tie up the wide skirt of my old ballerina dress, and we hike across the stones high above the water, looking for one smooth and flat enough to be our table. We set things up, and by the light of a candle burning in a pierced tin lantern, the Adriatic crashing and booming all around us, we eat quail stuffed with figs and girdled in pancetta and roasted on branches of sage, holding the birds in our hands, devouring the scant, sweet flesh down to the bone. We have a salad of fresh peas and butter lettuces and leaves of mint, all dressed in the quail-roasting juices, some good bread, and a cool Sauvignon from the Friuli. Is it really Prufrock sitting next to me, gently licking quail juices from his fingertips?

He sings "Nessuno al Mondo," and two fishermen who sit roast-ing clams and smoking pipes way below on the beach yell *bravo* up to the rocks. We talk about the wedding, and then Fernando tells me the story of the Festa della Sensa, the marriage of Venice to the sea. On the Feast of the Ascension, the anniversary of the day when the Virgin Mary was to have ascended into heaven, the doge, dressed as a bridegroom, would board the great gilt royal galley rowed by two hundred sailors and embark from the port on the Lido. A procession of flower-wreathed galleys and skiffs and gondolas rowed behind him until they reached San Nicolò, the point where the lagoon flows into the Adriatic. Then the patriarch stood on the prow and blessed the sea with holy water, while the doge cast his ring into the waves saying, "In sign of eternal dominion, I, who am Venice, marry you, O sea."

I like the symbolism, even if it is a bit of *hauteur,* that the doge "who is Venice" thinks he can tame the sea by marrying her, I tell Fernando. And did someone dive in to retrieve his ring, or did the pope give him a new one every year? I ask.

"I don't know about the ring, but I do know I'm wiser than the doges," he says, fiddling with the lantern, "and I would never think to tame you." Hmm, I wonder. I pull on my sweater and sip at my wine. I am happy to be marrying the stranger at this time in my life.

# 12

# A White Wool Dress Flounced in Twelve Inches of Mongolian Lamb

Whether we call it controlling or enabling or the more poetic "taming," power issues don't rear up as frenzied in a marriage between older people, the riper souls understanding these maneuvers to be ruinous. Older people get married for different reasons than young people do. Perhaps it's that in a younger partnership, the man lives on his side of the marriage and the woman on hers. Gracious opponents in competitions over career, social and economic status, frequency and intensity of applause, they meet at table or in bed, each exhausted from the solitary race. In a later marriage, even if they work on different things, they're still working as a team, remembering that being together was why they got married in the first place. I look at Fernando, and I can't imagine not remembering that.

And I can't imagine not remembering how Italians adore complication. A small farrago, some short agony, this they need every day. Less often, but often enough, it's a real chest-beating for which they yearn. A thing innocent of complication is not worth doing. Posting a letter and choosing a tomato are dramatic opportunities. Imagine then what stuff is a wedding. And not just any wedding, but a wedding to be designed and executed in six weeks, the wedding of an Italian man "of a certain age" to a foreign woman, also "of a certain age" who thinks of wearing a white wool dress flounced in twelve inches of Mongolian lamb at high mass. Ours is a wedding lavish with opportunity for complication. Opportunity number one: I wish to find a seamstress and get this mythical dress in the works.

The history of Venice has always been reflected in fabric. Look at the work of the Venetian Renaissance portrait painters. Light and fabric commandeer the eye; the subjects take second place. Look at Veronese and Longhi and Tintoretto and all three artists from the family Bellini. Look at Titian. One hears the rustle of a gown in yellow watered silk, one feels the deep cuts in the velvet of a sable-ruffled cape the color of pomegranates. Venetians told their story in brocade and lace and satin, in the length of a cuff woven from spun gold. A merchant's emporium, warehouse, and living quarters were all part of the same gilded palazzo, permitting him to move through each act of his day and night drenched in spectacle. Nobles, impoverished nobles, and often beggars dressed themselves in silk. "Why should one dress for misery?" is a query an old woman wrapped in ermine is said to have asked, as she sat each day begging in the Piazzetta. The Venetian twist on "Let them eat cake" was "Let us, at the very least, dress in silk."

Venetian painters dressed saints in satin and rarely let them go shoeless. Their Madonnas wore russet silk, or gold or royal blue; their coifs, jewels, slim waists detracted not at all from their hallowedness. Always nonintellectual, Venetians could not, still cannot be bothered by contradiction or duality. How can the mother of

Christ be dressed in taffeta and wear a ruby necklace at the foot of her son's cross? Venetians see it all as coexistence. In the end all that remains is the pageant, only the pageant, one allusive, artificial episode after another.

Venetians were, and some still are, astonished by themselves. That a silk-robed, clove-scented princess named Venice could be sprung from a swamp was a mad fancy. That she should flourish put her beyond myths and transfixed in these Venetians a sense that time is short. There is only here and only now, so let it all be picturesque inside the frolic and behind the mask.

Even if a few years have passed since then I hoped it would not be improbable to come across a nice length of soft, just-off-white wool, neither heavy nor thin, etched in some sort of delicate tracery, from which a silver-headed crone could stitch me a long, slim, white dress. I think it better to find first the crone, then the stuff.

Though there are dozens of listings in the phone directory under *sartoria,* tailor's shop, nearly every call is answered by someone saying, "Oh, that was my grandmother, *poveretta,* poor little thing, who passed away in eighty-one" or "My aunt, *poveretta,* who is blind thanks to fifty years of sewing sheets and underwear for the Borghesi."

When I find one, a man, still living and not blind, he barks, "I don't make wedding dresses."

"It's not a wedding dress I want but a dress I will wear at my wedding," I try to explain. A thought that makes perfect sense in English often travels poorly when translated literally into Italian, and the gruff voice wishes me a definitive good afternoon.

At last I find my *sarta,* a tinkling-voiced woman who says she's been making dresses for all the most beautiful Venetian brides since she was fifteen years old. She says two of hers were televised on Channel 5 and two more were photographed for Japanese magazines. Trying to calm her expectations I once again attempt the "It's not a wedding dress I want but a dress I will wear at my wedding" idea, but it fizzles as before. We make an appointment for *dialogo.*

Her atelier, a fifth-floor flat in Bacino Orseolo behind San Marco, overlooks the dock where waiting gondoliers gather to smoke and eat bread stuffed with mortadella and hustle up business. After drama with the buzzer and drama with her assistant, who does not want to admit me ten minutes early, I climb up to Rapunzel's tower. *La sarta* must not have been making wedding dresses for long, since she doesn't look much older than fifteen and her assistant looks twelve. They invite me to sit and look through a portfolio of drawings while I try to tell them I want a plain wool dress, good fabric, classic design. When I mention the Mongolian flounce I get their attention. *La sarta* begins to sketch on a tissue pad with a stub of pencil and in seconds there emerge the dress, a sort of cape, even a hat, a toque-like thing that would have been perfect for Gloria Swanson. "No," I tell them. "Simpler than that and with no cape, no hat. Just a dress."

*"Come vuole, signora.* As you wish," she says, edging her chin higher. She takes my measurements, hundreds of measurements. Knee to ankle, straight; knee to ankle, bent. Shoulders, standing; shoulders, sitting. The circumferences of wrist, middle forearm, elbow, upper arm. I feel like I'm being measured for embalming. She shows me bolt after bolt, swatch after swatch of gorgeous fabric, and when I

say I like something she tells me she doesn't have quite enough for the dress or that the house that makes that particular one is still closed for vacation so she can't yet try to order it and, even if she could contact them, she knows they haven't made that fabric for years and it's unlikely they'd have anything left. Why is she showing me things I can't have? Because what fun would it be if she had fifty yards of the fabric I wanted most in the world? What thrill would there be in that? No chafe, no twinge of anguish. It would end up being only a dress and not a wedding dress. "A little suffering sweetens things," she tells me.

I just sit there looking at her, thinking I am beginning to understand her, a fact that both terrifies and gladdens me. We settle on a piece of cashmere that feels like heavy silk. It is beautiful and just large enough. Bombastes asks the price and, of course, offends Rapunzel. She tells me to return in a week to discuss the *preventivo,* estimate, with her twelve-year-old assistant. Could I just telephone next week? "Signora, it's nicer if you can come here. The telephone is a little cold, no?" she corrects me again.

On my return, I climb up to the atelier, I sit and look at the embossed envelope with my name on it that sits in a tiny dish on the table before me. Do I pick it up and open it? Will the assistant read it to me? Do I take it home and read it and climb back up to the tower to say, okay? *La sarta* hands me the envelope and I feel free to look at the one line written on the paper inside. *Un abito di sposa*—seven million lire—about thirty-five hundred dollars at the current exchange rate. I could have two Romeo Gigli dresses plus Gucci boots plus lunch at Harry's once a week for a year for seven million lire. She sees my distress. I tell her the price is much more than I can pay, thank her for her time, and begin to back out the door. Even if the estimate was inflated just to see how much I would bear—a demonstration of *furbizia innocente*—I am appalled. I can only think that I have lost a precious week. Walking down and out into the piazza, I am sorry for the fifteen year old and the twelve year old that they must find someone else to pay their rent for the next three months.

I decide to forget the Mongolian flounce and just find a dress, readymade. I try Versace and Armani and Thierry Mugler. I try Biagiotti and Krizia. Nothing. One day I go to Kenzo in the Frezzeria, and as I leave the shop I pass by another called Olga Asta. Here the sign promises readymade as well as custom-made clothing. I tell the lady I am looking for a dress to wear to a wedding. Whose wedding I do not say. She shows me a string of *tailleurs*—nice little suits—one navy blue with a smart white shantung trim and a dark brown one with a matching silk blouse. All wrong and I am loath to even try them. I am already halfway through my exit song when she tells me she can make something for me, she can design and sew anything. Through a wince I ask, "What do you think about a simple white wool dress with a Mongolian flounce?"

"*Sarebbe molto bello, molto elegante, signora.* It would be very beautiful, very elegant," she says quietly. "We might even add a peplum to accentuate your waist." She shows me lengths of stuff actually sufficient to make a dress. We choose one, and then she asks me to wait while she climbs up to her atelier. It seems Olga Asta is also a furrier, and back down she comes with a hank of long white Mongolian lamb in a ruff round her neck. Motioning me to follow her out into the daylight, she shows me how the fur and the white wool are of the same creamy tint. "*Destino, signora, è proprio destino.* It is destiny, signora, absolute destiny." I want to know the price of destiny. Fearing inflation, I'm still mum about the fact that I'm to be the bride. She sits at her desk and writes and looks up prices and telephones upstairs to the atelier. Following decorum she does not announce the price aloud but writes two million lire on the back of her business card and hands it to me.

I say, *"Benone,"* just like Don Silvano and set up a series of appointments for fittings. I tell her the date on which I'll need the dress, and she flinches not at all.

I shake her hand and tell her how happy I am to have found her, and she says, *"Ma figurati.* Don't be silly, a bride-to-be must have exactly what she desires." I never asked how she knew I was the bride, but I was glad she did. After the third or fourth fitting, I ask her to just finish the dress. I am sure it will be perfect and will come to fetch it on the afternoon before the wedding. She agrees, and I wonder why everything can't be so clean and straight, and then I remember what Rapunzel told me and I am happy for the suffering that sweetens things.

⌒

Fernando decides the Hotel Bauer Grunewald will be the scene of our wedding lunch. His longtime friend and client Giovanni Gorgoni is the concierge there, and, early on, he told Fernando, *"Ci penso io.* I'll think of everything." So, according to the stranger, our reception is planned, a fait accompli.

"What is the menu?" seems a reasonable question from a bride who is a chef about her wedding lunch.

"It's a fabulous menu with hors d'oeuvres and Champagne on the terrace and five or six courses at table," he tells me, as though it was really information.

"*What* five or six courses?" I beg.

"It doesn't matter, it's the Bauer Grunewald, and everything will be wonderful," he says. I can't decide whether this is *bella figura* or *furbizia innocente* at work, but I would really like to meet with these folks who are to feed us on our wedding day. He says I worry too much, but if I'd like to see a copy of the menu, he'll ask Gorgoni for it. I want to tell him I've planned parties for Ted Kennedy and Tina Turner, but I don't. He'd tell me this is different. I know it's different, but I'd just like to be part of things.

One morning we meet by chance in Calle Larga XXII Marzo. He's just picked up the menu from the Bauer, and he hands it to me with great brio. It's an undusted fin de siècle beauty, full of odes to Rossini and Brillat-Savarin, and I see he has said yes to a fish course that raises the price of lunch by fifty percent, to three baked pasta dishes with the same sauce, to "house wines" without knowing from whose house they will come, and a wedding cake sullied with a plastic gondola. I feel my sabre rattling. I look a little off to the left as I tell him *I* want to cater our wedding. Does he want to see my menu? He rolls his eyes until I think he's going to have a fit, and I crumple the menu and stuff it in my purse. I have one more bullet.

"Wouldn't it be lovely to have something a little less formal? We could all go out to Torcello and sit under the trees at Diavolo." I'm thinking of my sweet waiter with the salmon-colored cravat and the pomaded hair parted in the middle, the same waiter who brought us cherries in iced water at the end of our first lunch together on

Torcello. The stranger kisses me hard and long on the lips, leaves me standing in the middle of the *calle,* and heads back toward the bank's main office for a meeting. I know the kiss says I love you with my whole heart, and I know too that it says we will not traipse out to Torcello with the priest and the pageboys and Armenian monks and a delegation from the British Women's Club to sit under the trees and be served by the waiter with the salmon-colored cravat. Most clearly of all it says you will not cook for your own wedding.

Why do I let him dismiss me like this? Without deciding to, I step inside Venezia Studium and buy a small, pleated white silk pouch finished with a tassle and suspended from a long satin cord. At least I can decide what purse I'll carry to my wedding lunch. I feel better, my perspective back in focus. The marriage is more important than the event to me, and I know that's why I just let the stranger fly. And besides, he's having so much fun. Anyway, if the Bauer's propaganda is at all true, even the Aga Khan and Hemingway suffered through the same bloody meal.

∽

Fernando asks me to meet him one morning at a travel agency where he has already booked us on the night train to Paris. "Why do we have to go to Paris on a honeymoon when we live in Venice?" I ask him.

"It is precisely because we live in Venice that we are going to Paris," he says.

My big job is to choose the hotel. When he tells me we're going to the printer's to look at paper and typeface for our invitations, I can't believe it. We're inviting nineteen people!

"I'll get some wonderful paper and envelopes and use my calligraphy pens. We can use wax and a seal, if you'd like. They'll be personal and beautiful," I tell him.

"*Troppo artigianale.* Too homemade," he says.

The printer's workshop is an ink-smudged dream scented with hot metal and new paper, and I could stay there forever. The printer sets stacks of albums before us and says, "*Andate tranquilli.* Take your time." We look through all the books, and then we look through all the books again and the stranger places his finger on a page full of engravings of Venetian barques. He likes one with a couple being rowed down the Grand Canal. I like it too, and so we order it in a dark Venetian red on woven silky paper of the palest green. We go to take an espresso at Olandese Volante while the printer prepares the estimate. When we return, the printer is off working and a little folded-up piece of paper addressed to us waits on his desk. The cost will be six hundred thousand lire. That's three hundred dollars for nineteen invitations. When the printer comes back to us he is apologetic for the cost and explains that the lowest amount of paper he can order is for 150 invitations. Even though we need only nineteen, we must pay for 150.

"Let's choose another paper," I say.

"But the lowest lot is always 150," says the printer.

"I understand. But surely another paper might be less costly," I try. The stranger is not budging. He wants the dark red boat on the pale green sea for six hundred thousand.

"Okay, then let's take all 150," I suggest.

"And what will we do with 150 invitations?" Fernando counters.

I look to the printer for solution, but he is shaking his head in despair.

"Can't you just print nineteen or twenty-five or something like that and leave the rest blank so we can use them as notecards?" I ask gingerly. He doesn't understand my question. I revert to charades. Fernando lights a cigarette under the No Smoking sign.

Finally the printer says, *"Certo, certo, signora, possiamo fare così."* I am amazed he has said yes. Fernando is close to angry that I asked for something so extrordinary. He says I am *incorreggibile.* He says I am like Garibaldi in eternal revolt.

All we have left to think about are rings and flowers and music.

One night we ride across the water to meet with an organist who lives near the Sottoportego de le Acque, a whisper away from Il Gazzettino. I like the circle I'm making. Il Gazzettino was my first Venetian hotel, and now I'm about to climb the stairs next door to see the man who will play Bach at my wedding. When I mention this to the stranger, all he says is "Bach?" We ring the bell and meet Giovanni Ferrari's father, who thrusts his head out the second-floor window and tells us to come up, that his son is still with a student. Papà Ferrari looks like an old doge, locks of wild white hair escaping from his tight wool cap, his neck and shoulders muffled in a big paisley shawl. It is the end of September and nearly balmy outdoors.

Two candles burn on the mantle of a fireplace. I love that these are the only light in the great salon. As my eyes adjust, I see that sheet music is helter-skelter, everywhere. It sits in precarious piles on chairs and sofas; boxes of it line the walls and block pathways. The old doge floats off into some other room without saying anything more, and so we just stand there in the candlelight among Frescobaldi and Froberger, being careful not to trip over Bach. I gasp when Giovanni comes out from his studio.

He is the old doge in youth. Or is it the same man in a slightly changed costume? The same long thin face, with the same high-arched nose, wool cap, scarf, he says how pleased he will be to play for us, that we must only select the pieces. By now I know better than to think he really means there is some choice in the matter. The stranger is getting ready to dance with him, and I just watch and listen. Giovanni asks what we would like, and the stranger says we have complete faith in his taste; he says it is traditional to play such and such, and the stranger ends with, "Of course, those are exactly what we'd hoped for all along." Quick, smooth, conventional. Each one has saved the other's face as well as his own. No one talked about money. This is a world away from any other world, I think as we walk back in the silence of the Sottoportego.

I remember this silence and the horrid hotel and Fiorella's smile and running up and down over a hundred bridges in my thin snake-skin sandals. During that time in Venice, it was as though Fiorella was trying to mother me. "Sei sposata? Are you married?" she wanted to know.

I told her I was divorced, and she clicked her tongue. "You shouldn't be alone," she said.

"I'm not alone, just not married, that's all," I told her.

"But you shouldn't be traveling alone," she pressed.

"I've been traveling alone since I was fifteen."

She clicked her tongue again and as I turn to leave she said, "*In fondo, sei triste*. Deep down, you're sad."

I didn't have the language to tell her it wasn't sadness she sensed in me. Only my separateness. Even in English it's difficult to trans-late "separateness." I broadened my grin, but she was still looking beyond it. I raced off, and she yelled at my shoulders, *"Allora, sei almeno misteriosa.* Well then, at the least, you're mysterious."

I look up to the window on whose sill I sat on that long ago and first afternoon. I ask the stranger to stand there under the window with me, to hold me.

# 13

# Here Comes the Bride

We choose very wide wedding bands, brushed gold, heavy, wonderful. And the florist is so excited about us wanting baskets rather than vases of flowers that she takes me to a warehouse down by the train station where we find six white-washed Sicilian beauties, tall, with arched handles. She says she will fill them with whatever is most beautiful in the markets on the morning of the wedding. She says the Madonna will see to it that we have magnificent flowers. I like that she and the Madonna operate on such a familiar basis. I ask if she thinks the Madonna might send a few golden Dutch iris on October 22. She kisses me three times. I begin to wonder if this exchange has been too simple and if I'm having too little suffering. But on the day before the wedding the stranger provides.

It is nearly time to meet him at the bank, and I have already gone to collect my dress and the lacy stockings I'd ordered at Fogal. I'd also decided to take the white tulle bustier I'd been eyeing at Cima. The tribe at the market and Do Mori staged a sort of bridal shower for me this morning, and so my market sack is full of roses and chocolates and lavender soaps and six newspaper-wrapped eggs from the egg lady, who also offered precise instructions that Fernando and I should each drink three of them, raw and beaten up with a dose of grappa, for strength. I'd gone to sit at Florian for a while, and the bartender there, Francesco, introducing his latest cocktail, passed round a taste to everyone in the little bar. Vodka and cassis and white grape juice. They said *auguri* so many times I was embarrassed, and when they said, "We'll see you tomorrow," I think they meant they would see us here in the piazza when the stranger and I and the wedding party make the traditional promenade through Venice.

As I walk to meet Fernando, I notice something is missing: I can hardly remember the last time I felt the weight of the pest on my heart. Sometime over the last month or so I'd left it behind, confounded it for good. Or is that I've just passed it onto Fernando?

When we meet, the stranger is pale, his eyes are fixed in his well-practiced dying-bird stare. I must remind myself he is only being Italian. On this day before his wedding, surely he is due his quotient of angst. He doesn't ask about my dress or my day or my sackful of roses. He doesn't even look at me. I think it's just jitters, and so I say, "Would you like to be alone for a while?"

"Absolutely not," he answers almost in a whisper, as though I'd suggested he take a walk over glowing coals.

"Would you like to go home and take a long bath and I'll fix you a *camomilla?*" I try again. He just shakes his head. "Are you sad we're getting married?" I ask him.

"How can you say such a thing?" he says, eyes flashing back to life. He is quiet on the *motonave* and doesn't break his silence even as we walk. When we reach the corner of the Gran Viale and Via Lepanto, he says, "I can't go home with you right now. There are some things I have left to do. Cesana forgot to write us in and now he can't make

it tomorrow because he has another wedding. I have to talk to someone else." Cesana was to be our photographer, another old friend
and client who had said, *"Ci penso io.* Leave it to me."

"Is that what's making you so desperate?" I ask

He shrugs but doesn't answer. I tell him we can always find someone to take a few pictures, but he will not be comforted. "And I
haven't yet gone to confession," he says. He begins a convulsive defense. "I've been meaning to go for weeks but I just never found the
right moment. I don't believe in confession and absolution, anyway,"
he says. He is justly uneasy, I think, since thirty years have slipped
away since he's heard the awful sliding of a confessional screen, but
it was he who wanted all this, he who reinvented the truth to make
it all happen, and now, seventeen hours before the ceremony, it's
dogma he wants to discuss? I say nothing because he is talking
enough for both of us. When he's finally quiet, I say I'll go on ahead
to the dacha and wait for him.

"I'll have tea and a bath ready," I offer once again.

"I told you, I don't want tea or a bath," he says, a little too loudly
and leaves me holding tight to the wedding dress and the roses. I
change and run down to the beach, trying to understand what it was
he couldn't say. After a while, he comes loping along and we sit on
the sand, legs tangled and facing each other.

"Old ghosts?" I want to know.

"Very old ghosts," he says, "and none of whom I invited to my
wedding."

"Gone back where they belong?" I ask.

*"Si. Si, sono tutti andati via.* Yes. Yes, all of them gone away," he tells
me as though it's true. *"Perdonami.* Forgive me."

"Wasn't it you who told me there isn't an agony in the world as powerful as tenderness?" I ask.

"Yes, and I know it's true," he says pulling me up to my feet.

"I'll race you down to the Excelsior. We'll have our last glass of wine as sinners. Wait a minute. I just went to confession. Does this mean we can't sleep together tonight?" he asks.

"Let's call Don Silvano and let him decide," I say over my shoulder, getting a head start on the race.

He still gets to the hotel first and holds his arms out to catch me, kissing me and kissing me so I can hardly catch my breath.

"Do you remember the first moment when you knew you loved me?" he asks.

"Not exactly the *first* moment. But I think it might have been when you walked into the living room from your bath the night you arrived in Saint Louis. I think it was the knee socks and the slicked-back hair," I tell him.

"I know when it happened to me. It was on the first day I saw you in Vino Vino. As I walked back to my office from the restaurant, I tried to put your face together in my mind but I couldn't do it. After all those months of seeing your profile almost every time I closed my eyes, I couldn't find you. I dialed that number and asked to speak to you, but I had no idea what I wanted to tell you. All I knew was that when I looked at you I didn't feel cold anymore. I didn't feel cold anymore."

⌒

We had decided the most romantic thing would be to get up with the sun on our wedding day, to walk along the sea together, to drink coffee, to separate, and meet in church. Days before, we arrange it all with the concierge at the little hotel next door to our building, telling him Fernando needs to rent a room for half a day. The concierge asks no questions. The stranger takes his clothes and an overnight bag and sets out along the ten yards past the troll to the hotel. The whole thing feels silly and strange and exciting. I go off to Giulio, the hairdresser on the Gran Viale and ask him to make tight ringlets all over my head with a curling iron. *"Sei pazza?* Are you crazy? All this beautiful hair. Let me do something classic, a chignon, an upsweep with these antique combs," he says flailing two huge picks laid with fake stones that are less antique than he. "No, I just want curls, and I'll do the rest," I tell him. It takes more than two hours, and he has mourned each squeezing of the hot, steaming contraption. When he finishes, I look like Harpo Marx, but I say, "Fine," and he says *Che disperazione.* How hopeless." He gives me an old blue scarf to cover my head for the walk home.

I am wishing that Lisa and Erich were with me. Erich had spent August with us, he and I racing about the islands, eating veal cutlets and drinking icy wine at every lunch, staying hours inside Palazzo Grassi and behaving as though we were on vacation together, as we did when he and Lisa were younger. Lisa has been sweet, supportive, but she has kept apart. My whirling about during those last months in America exhausted both my children, especially Lisa. By this time in a life, mothers are supposed to have settled down, *mellowed,* accepted their lives. Here I was, going the other way, tearing everything apart, packing it all up, and starting yet once again. I was always gypsy mom. And now, I'm gypsy mom in a gondola. I think it was also the pure speed at which everything unrolled. It's one thing to follow a Venetian, and another to marry him four months later.

"Why can't you wait at least until Christmas?" Lisa asked.

"I can't, honey. Fernando arranged everything so quickly there wasn't really an opportunity to consider your schedules. Things are different here. And because I don't speak the language very well yet and because of the bureaucratic miasma, I just didn't have very much to say about when or where," I said.

I know how weak this summary is, how uncharacteristically powerless I sound. Wimp, gypsy mom in a gondola. As I walk up the stairs to the apartment and run my bath and begin to dress, the ache for them, the longing to look at them, to touch them, comes in great heaving paroxysms. I should be walking down the aisle with them; we should be marrying the stranger together.

I push my hair up at the nape of my neck and secure it high on the crown of my head with barrettes to which the florist has attached red sweetheart roses and baby's breath, all of which tumble and tangle among the softening black curls. I leave the ringlets at the sides to hang as they will, thinking it's all very French Empire. The old baroque pearls go in my ears, and I'm ready to get into my dress. I step into it and pull it up around my hips—good. I begin sliding in my arms, but they move into the sleeves only halfway. Something must be stuck, a thread must need cutting. I examine the sleeves, and there is nothing amiss except that they are an inch too narrow to contain my arms. Do I have fat arms? I do not have fat arms. If anything, they tend toward thinness. La signora Asta must have had a vision while she was finishing the sleeves. Now what do I do? I begin mentally searching the armoire. What do I have that I could pretend I intended to wear to my wedding? There's a white satin slip dress but no jacket, and that would be a scandal at high mass—and anyway it's October out there. There's the lavender silk taffeta with the bustle and the train and all the poufs that I bought in the fifth-floor designer close-out salon in the Galleries Lafayette in 1989, just in case I was ever invited to a ball. This is not a ball. I run to find the body oil to rub on my arms to make them slippery but I can't find the body oil, so I use olive oil, extra virgin, but it doesn't help much. I am crying and laughing and trembling, still wondering why I am alone. Some princess I am, with no one near to help me. God help me. It's my wedding day.

It requires a Houdini sort of shimmying, but finally the dress is zipped and though I cannot raise my arms beyond my waist, I think it's beautiful. I spray Opium on my arms to cover the scent of olive oil, and I'm ready. One tiny detail we seem to have overlooked. How will I get to the church? So elementary is this question we have forgotten it altogether. There is no posied chariot to take me to my wedding and I would walk, but I know Fernando would be horrified. I dial for the taxi and head down the stairs past the troll and out under the gallery of yellowing elms. I sing "Here Comes the Bride," but I don't cry.

I have always understood that the bride should not enter the church until all the guests are inside. In Italy it is, quite naturally, the opposite. The groom and the wedding party wait inside, the guests wait outside to greet the bride and follow her inside the church. I

am making the *tassista,* the lady taxi driver, nervous because I am a
bride, and she feels the responsibility as she might for a birthing
mother and, too, because I refuse to get out of her car until no more
guests are standing outside the church. She never says a word that
might help me to understand Italian custom. She only drives. She is
a very small woman and her head, when she is ensconced behind the
wheel, is flush with the seatback. Each time I tell her I can't yet stop
in front of the church, that she must make another turn around the
block until the guests are all inside, she slides a little further down
on the seat until her arms are stretched up almost straight and her
head is not visible at all. Another *giro.* Another *giro.* Finally there is
no one left outside the church. The *tassista,* verbal at last, says that's
because they probably all went home. But I am satisfied. I step from
the taxi and up to the church doors. I can't get them opened, the
damn medieval things. Stuck shut they seem, and my sleeves are so
tight I can't raise my arms to get a good grip. I put my flowers down
on the steps, yank open the doors, pick up my flowers, walk through
the tiny vestibule and come upon my wedding.

"*Lei è arrivata.* She's arrived," I hear whispered everywhere.
Giovanni Ferrari caresses Bach up from the organ. The white-washed
baskets are full of pink hydrangea and red roses and golden Dutch
iris, which I know have come directly from the Madonna. The air
is opal twilight blazing with the flames of a hundred white candles
and a single dazzle of sun from the lapis lazuli window. Two black-
bearded Armenian monks in silver silk robes are chanting, swinging
pots of frankincense and sending thick musky plumes floating up
over the altar, and I think this church is another room in my house.

Everything is misty through tears that won't fall, and the only person I see clearly is Emma from the British Women's Club in turban and pearls. Two hired pageboys in white britches and stiff pink jackets bestrew rose petals before me, and I walk slowly, very slowly, toward the blueberry-eyed stranger standing there in swallow tails in the frankincense fog.

Don Silvano holds out two hands to me. He bends down and says, *"Ce l'abbiamo fatta.* We did it." This is a gesture of welcome, of affection, a gift to me, I think, and perhaps a quiet message to the curious Lidensi who have filled the little church to its rafters, who have come to see *l'americana* be wedded to one of them. The tears are free now and, weeping, I sit next to the stranger, also weeping, on a red velvet sofa. Neither of us can really look at the other for fear of some greater weeping, but when we say our vows we look anyway, weep anyway. Giovanni is playing "Ave Maria" and Don Silvano is crying, too. Is he thinking of Santa Maria della Salute, I wonder?

*"Una storia di vero amore"* he says, as he presents us to the congregation. Giovanni cries and plays as though he is Lohengrin himself, and all the faces we pass along the aisles are wet and shiny and shouting *"Ecco gli sposi, viva gli sposi.* There's the bride and groom, long live the bride and groom." I hadn't seen them in the church, but there outside the door is a contingent of Venetians who came over the water to see us be married. People from the shops, staff from Florian, chums from Do Mori and the market, a librarian from the Venetian National Library, one of the threadbare *contessas* who is a client of the bank, the *sarta* who had the vision while she was finishing my sleeves. Even Cesana is there, snapping away, and everyone is crying and

throwing pasta and rice and my husband, who was once the stranger, is slapping at the pockets of his gray velvet vest trying to find a cigarette. I think, perhaps, this is how the world should end.

On the ride in the water taxi, we sit outside as we did that first day we met when Fernando rode with me to the airport in breezes blowing just as cool. I pull the same little glass out of its velvet pouch, pour out cognac from the same silver flask. We sip, and the boat lurches and slaps down through the lagoon, the water spraying our faces just barely dried of tears. Cesana directs the water-taxi driver to stop on the island of San Giorgio for photographs, and Fernando slips one leg, up to the knee, into the lagoon. Cesana shoots the scene. We debark in the Bauer canal, step directly into the wedding gondola and are rowed back out into the Grand Canal. Trailing us in another gondola, the great-girthed Cesana leans and wobbles and shoots. Our gondolier shouts to Cesana, "Where shall I go?" Cesana tells him to follow the sun.

Guests on the terraces of Hotel Europa e Regina and the Monaco, as well as our own at the Bauer, wave and shout, and for a moment I float above the little tableau, believing, not believing it is my tableau. This is happening to all of us, I think. This wedding, these spangles of sunlight, this glissade through blue water, the old sweet faces of the palazzi looking down, this pink-washed peace is for all of us. This is for every one of us who was ever lonely. How I wish I could give away pieces of this day like loaves of warm bread.

The call has gone out to all the gondolas in that part of the canal to gather in front of the Bauer, and soon eighteen, twenty boats have made a circle around us. The gondoliers serenade us and their passengers, who thought only of a ride down the canal but find themselves instead a chorus in the spectacle of a wedding.

It is magnificent out on the hotel terrace, but we are invited inside into a plain white room with no windows, where there are no flowers, where there is no music, for a lunch that no one, save Cesana and the silver-robed monks, really eats. I think of Hemingway and the Aga Khan.

It is ancient Venetian custom for a bride and groom, priest and, sometimes, wedding party to walk from church to reception and back to the bride's house, passing along the way those people and places that have been and will continue to be their life, the priest officially presenting them to their city as husband and wife. Because we live on the beach rather than in the city, we choose to stroll from the Bauer down Salizzada San Moisè into Piazza San Marco and, finally, out to Riva Schiavoni and the boat back home.

I begin to say good-bye to people outside the Bauer, but soon I understand that no one is leaving us. Our guests, the two pageboys, Emma, arm in arm with the two monks, Don Silvano, Cesana, and, now, Gorgoni, the Bauer's concierge, will walk in formation with us on our wedding day. I think we are a beautiful parade. As we come through Ala Napoleonica, the orchestra at Florian stops mid-song and begins to play "Lili Marlene," and by the time we are all there in front of the café the orchestra has begun the "Walzer dell' Imperatore." It is five in the afternoon, and every table outdoors is full. People are on their feet snapping photos, shouting, "Dance, you must dance." And so we dance. All of Venice must be here in this great crowd around us, and I wish we could all dance together. My husband is holding me, and I think, no, *this* is the way the world should end.

As we are walking away, a woman steps into our path. In Italian heavily accented in French she says, "Thank you for giving me the Venice I had hoped to find." She is gone before I can respond.

Having stayed too long at our own wedding, back home we have minutes to prepare ourselves for the ride to Santa Lucia to catch the eight-forty train to Paris. I pull the rose-covered combs from my hair and stuff them inside *Larousse,* where they are still. Jeans, a short black cashmere sweater, black leather jacket for me. Fernando keeps his tuxedo shirt, adds jeans and his old flight jacket. I grab my bouquet, and we're off again on the water. Francesco is at the train gate to wave us off, to hand me our wedding gift. We board in a confusion of smoke and rain, and I see that same French woman who spoke to us on the piazza racing by. She waves and grins. Fernando says he hopes the pageboys and Emma and the monks have not decided to follow us to Paris. We find our compartment, heave in our bags, and close the door behind us as the train begins to chug-chug away to France. "We're married!" we scream.

We are also exhausted. I strip down to my white lace bustier and climb up into bed while Fernando lights a candle. Two minutes after he's settled up there with me, he says, "I'm hungry. I'm so hungry I won't be able to sleep. I'll have to get dressed and go out to the dining car."

"Better yet," I tell him, "look inside the carry-on bag." Francesco had packed up two dozen tiny sandwiches—thin curls of roasted ham on soft oval rolls with sweet butter—and a big sack of crinkle-cut potato chips, and half a Sacher torte. He'd stuffed a bottle of Piper Heidsick in a vacuum bag with four ice packs. Glasses, napkins. When he'd asked me what I wanted for a wedding present, I'd told him it was this exact supper I wished for and that if he could bring it to the station when he came to see us off, it would be the perfect gift. Fernando unzips the bag and says, "I love you."

We spread everything out on the bottom bunk, and we eat and drink and climb back up top. Finally I know the real way the world should end.

# 14

# I Just Wanted to Surprise You

We are barely awake when the train pulls into the Gare de Lyon. I pull on my jeans, pull a hat over yesterday's curls, grab my bouquet, and follow Fernando out and up into the station. We have bowls of café au lait and croissants, warm, each one a thousand buttery crumbs, filling my mouth. I don't know how many I eat, because I decide to stop counting after three. We are racing out the door into the Sunday Paris light, and we hear, *"Les fleurs, les fleurs, madame."* I'd left my bouquet on the bar, and who was there to find it and run after me but that same French woman.

That same French woman must also live in the Latin Quarter where we are staying at Hotel des Deux Mondes because we see her at every turn. She is at Café de Flore in the morning, feeding bits of a jambon beurre to her fluff of a puppy on a leash, and she smiles and nods but never more than that. At five she is already sitting outdoors at Les Deux Magots with a glass of red wine, a little dish of *picholine* olives, the electric heaters tucked into the awnings warming her. We sit outside, too, sipping at Ricard, welcoming the evening. It seems everything she wants us to understand is contained in those gestures of smiling and nodding and as though she needs to know nothing more about us than she does already. We like having her nearby, and she seems to like having us nearby, and therein is benevolence.

Our days are undesigned. We walk until we see something we'd like to see more closely, and then we walk again until we want to sit or go back to bed or go early to lunch at Toutone so we can go late to lunch at Bofinger or to lunch not at all, so we can go at eight to Balzar for oysters and then to Le Petit Zinc for mussels at midnight. We crisscross the sprawl of Paris again and again, as though she were a tiny parish. When we run into our French woman at Museé d'Orsay, it seems strange enough, but when we find ourselves side by side with her in the Egyptian exhibition at the Louvre, I begin to think our meetings spookish. When she is already drinking tea at Ladurée in the Rue Royale as we come in for ours, I can't decide who is following whom. Is she a Parisian keeper of the newly wedded, assigned to us for the honeymoon? Is that why she was there in the piazza when we waltzed on our wedding day? I wish one of us would say something about this chapter of accidents and flukes, but none of us does. When a day passes without seeing her, I begin to miss her. "How can you miss someone you don't know?" Fernando asks. When two or three days more pass without seeing her I know we've lost her forever, or that perhaps she was simply some druidess figment, fond of middle-aged brides and waltzes and tiny green olives.

We have stayed a long time in Paris, a month of days and nights inside the rapture. Because it's nearly time to return to Venice, I begin to wonder how that will feel. "Fernando, what do you think will happen when we return home?"

"Nothing so different," he tells me. "We're our own happiness. We're the festival, and wherever we go our life won't change much. Different backdrops, different people, always us," he says, with eyes that look straight ahead but sneak back to check my response to his broad brush. Is he trying to tell me something without telling me again? What's he saving up for me, behind that jauntiness? We decide to fly back to Venice rather than ride the train, and in the airport we see that same French woman in line for a flight to London. With my eyes I say thank you for her gentle chaperoning through these first days of marriage and she, with hers, says it's been a pleasure. I can't help but wonder about her next assignment, about the lucky couple to whom she'll flash the silky comfort of that goddess smile. And, I wonder, too, about her finding real *picholine* in London.

It is November 21, and we are just awakening to our first morning back from Paris. I remember this is the Festa di Santa Maria della Salute, the feast recording the day when Doge Nicolò Contarini declared to the Venetians that, after twelve years of ravaging, the black death had been extinquished by a miracle of the Madonna. I want to attend services, to offer a new Venetian's thanks to the Madonna and others, not only for past miracles but also for their unwitting role in convincing Don Silvano to marry us last month. I ask Fernando if he'd like to go, too, but he says the bank reentry promises enough ritual observance. I tell him I'll go alone, that I'll meet him at home for dinner.

On this day each year, six or eight gondolas perform as *traghetti,* transfer vessels, to ferry the celebrants back and forth across the canal from Santa Maria del Giglio to the Salute. I arrive at four and queue for the *traghetto* among quiet, almost orderly crushes of people who overload the landing stage. Almost all of them are women, and they stand up in the *traghetto,* twelve, fifteen of them at a time, tottering, leaning against one another and, without apology, casually linking arms to steady themselves. When it's my turn I see that the gondolier who is hoisting people down onto the floor of the boat turns out to be my very own, my wedding-day gondolier and he lifts me in a wide arc from the dock down into the boat, saying *"Auguri e bentornata.* Greetings and a good homecoming to you." Venice is a small town, after all. And now it's my small town. The older ladies in the *traghetto* beam at this expression of *allegria* and, once I'm settled into the boat, I link arms, too, as though I link arms always. There is a sympathy out here on the wavy black water, in the rocking black boat.

We debark in front of the basilica, and I stand a while looking at her, lit as she is by the wake of powdered yellow light the sun just left behind. Raised up at the apex of the half-circle formed between San Marco and the Redentore on the Giudecca, Longhena's great church rests upon a million wooden pilings sunk into the mud bottom of the lagoon. Round and immense and sullen, too big for her throne, she seems a grand robust queen sitting in a dainty garden. What conceit had a man to dream this temple, to suppose he could build it and then do it? I walk over to the narrow pontoon bridge that is flung out across the canal only on this one day each year. Venetians negotiate its swinging, shifting platforms, carrying gifts in thanks to this Madonna, who delivered their ancestral families from the plague nearly five hundred years ago. Once the offerings were loaves of bread or cakes stuffed with fruits, jam or salted fish, maybe a sack of fat, red beans. Now the pilgrims bring candles, each holding one like a prayer, the flames of the faithful lighting up the cold stones of the Virgin's old house. Near the steps of the basilica, I buy a candle, a thick white one whose breadth is nearly too big for my hand to grasp. Without my asking, a woman lights my candle with the flame of hers. She smiles and melts into the crowds.

Generations of women walk together, sometimes three or four sets of linked lives, their connections chiseled into their flesh by the same artist. An old woman walks with her daughter, her grand-daughter, her great-granddaughter, and I see the baby girl's face in the great-grandmother's face. The old woman's legs, sticks in white stockings, are brittle, tentative under a pretty red wool coat. What's her story? She wears a beret pulled low over straight silver hair. The woman who is her daughter has hair straight and silver, too, and the one who is *her* daughter has hair straight and blond. One of them has pulled the baby girl's beret low over *her* blond head, and the four of them are beautiful. This is what I've always wanted, I think as I watch them. I've wanted to belong, to matter, to cherish and be cherished. I wanted life to be that romantic, that simple and safe. Is it ever that way? Is anyone ever sure? I wish my daughter was walking over this bridge now. I wish I was waiting for her. I would like to hear her voice, to hear our voices together in the dusky blue of this twilight, on our way to visit the Madonna. I would like to tell my daughter that she can be sure.

Inside, the basilica is a great ice cave draped in red velvet. The air is blue from the perishing cold, cold like the oldest cold, five centuries of cold trapped in white marble. No room to move, all of us touch, our breath blowing out in smoky clouds. Bishops and priests stand at every altar blessing the faithful, aspergillums of holy water lifted high above their heads. I try to move closer to a small side altar where a very young priest exuberantly sprinkles the congregation. Perhaps it is his first festival of the Salute, as it is mine, and I think his benediction would be particularly fitting. Feet swaddled in woolen socks, legs in thick suede boots to the knee, long shawl over long coat over long dress, Fernando's World War II cossack hat with the earflaps down, I am Mother Russia, and still I am cold. I wonder how it must feel to be Venetian, to be part of this rite, to know that one's blood and bones are descended from the blood and bones of those who have lived and died here for so long. How little I know about myself, I think, as I walk back down the steps and over to the *traghetto*.

I see him then, beaver hat, long green Loden cape slung over his shoulders, looking like Caesar on the Rubicon. Quickly, I remember something I *do* know about myself. I know that I love this man with my whole heart. My husband steps up from the boat. "There you are," he says. "I wanted to surprise you." As if the idea of surprising me was just revealed to him.

~

Fernando is right in that nothing is so different in our post-marriage-posthoneymoon-in-Paris-settled-back-in-Venice life, nothing much, except he is hardly ready to live quietly ever after. He says it's time we began the real work on the apartment. I'm feeling a Paris sheen and noticing a slowly growing comfort in the rhythms of my Venetian life. I have even grown affectionate toward the draped ruins and, at least for now, I am not convinced we must begin tearing apart the walls. He says winter is the right time to do it, that waiting at all means waiting another year, and that's too long. I prefer to wait. I want to think about Christmas and then about spring. I tell him that I just want to live in peace and without a major project.

He says that's just fine as long as I understand that the restructuring is inevitable. "We can't pretend that just because it *looks* so beautiful in here right now all the structural work doesn't matter anymore." He's right. And I know that somehow he feels a connection between the work on the apartment and his own personal weeding and scrubbing and that's why he doesn't want to wait. Exhilarated by the momentum of these past months, Fernando wants more of it. "It's your project, though," he tells me one evening, as though he is conceding Austria. "So you'll have to decide when to begin."

"At the least, let's get the plan on paper," I say, and so we write a list, room by room, meter by meter, of each phase of the work to be done. I see the extent of the whole tantalizing plot in black and white, and not even a minute passes before I feel the primal whip of the fire keepers. Since the beginning of forever, I have always seen to it that the larder was fat and the table serene. But fire keepers are also in charge of fixing up the house. Or, in my case, in charge of watching over those who fix up the house. And the next house, and the one after that. Without even applying, I've got my old job back, and I tell Fernando I'm ready.

I spend my afternoons looking at fixtures and appliances and tile and such, getting estimates for various parts of the work. In the evening Fernando and I go together to these suppliers, make final selections and contract the work. I try not to replay the laments and desperate tales of every foreigner who ever negotiated more than the dry cleaning of a raincoat in Italy. Those overblown stories about the everyday machinations of the Italian worker are the stuff of slapstick. Haven't I just passed through the wickets all the way to my wedding? Still there is some uneasiness about this journey into the jackhammering of what's left of the bathroom floor. I must remember that not only am I in Italy, I am in Venice, and surely the Princess will present a piquancy all her own.

The first thing to learn is that the whole Venetian enterprise is water-dependent. Venice was raised up a refuge, her inaccessability is her very reason to be. Not so much has changed over fifteen centuries, in that nothing can take the old girl by surprise. Everything and everyone travels her shimmery domain by boat. Even those persons and goods that would come upon her by air must then be plied over the water. Hence there is a surcharge on every potato, every nail and sack of flour, every lightbulb and flat of petunias for passage across the lagoon and canals. For travelers as well as citizens, Venice is the most expensive city in Italy, a fact justified by her watery situation, the same position that grants immunity to all lateness. Who is fool enough to argue with *"La barca è in ritardo.* The boat is late," or *"C'era nebbia.* There was fog"? Even homegrown goods must traverse a canal or two, a *rio,* a *riello.* Water is the conduit, water is the barrier, and Venetians use both to their advantage. The woodworker who comes to replace a floorboard or the cement-dusted squad that comes to resurface your walls—all chant the water theme, and this affects how things get done.

We lose the first two weeks in January to "fog," the third to "high water," the fourth to "humidity." On the last day of the month, work begins. That is, the tools of the preliminary destruction are delivered and the workers tramp from room to room, knocking on the

walls, measuring, shaking heads, rolling eyes. It's not as though they
haven't seen the job, studied the situation, approved the plans, but
still they pace about like commanders in a war room. Their preferred way to smoke is to wedge a lit stick in the corner of the
mouth and let it be. They talk, sneer, get on with things while the
cigarette burns down to a long snake of undisturbed ash. Then they
remove the butt of it and crush it under their heel. After all, isn't the
floor going to be replaced?

And yet despite such a stammering start, work proceeds nicely,
even steps up toward briskness, with the men singing and whistling,
their smoldering cigarettes all the while secure between their lips.
When these men work, they work hard and well, but they are
sprinters with no predisposition for long distance. After three hours
each day, they're at the finish line. Somehow the destruction phase
eases into the reconstruction phase, and I'm thinking it's going fairly
well until I notice Fernando shuffling through the rubble on his way
to the bedroom one evening. I already understand that the *process*
terrifies him. He won't be happy until the work is finished and at
least twelve people have told him it's magnificent. But there he is,
lying crosswise on the bed, dead-bird eyes cast up, saying he just
doesn't like the damn apartment and nothing we do to improve it is
going to make much difference to him.

"It's small and cramped and there's no light and we're spending all
this money for nothing," he tells me.

"It's small and cramped and there's no light and we're spending all
this money, but it's *not* for nothing. You're the one who insisted we
take the place down to its ribs. I don't understand you," I tell him,
wishing I could be alone in a room with no sledgehammer, no buck-

ets. Not a single bag of cement. No stranger. "Why don't we just sell the place?" I take him by surprise. "Is there a *sestiere* in Venice where you'd like to live? Surely, if we tried, we could find an apartment, with a *mansarda,* a roof-top space, that we could fix up and *both* grow to love," says the gypsy in me. My proposal disturbs him.

"Do you know the cost of real estate in Venice?" he asks.

"About the same as the cost of real estate on the Lido, most likely. Why don't we go to see an agent and just get a reading on the market?" I ask.

He repeats "real estate agent" in the same tone he might say "Antichrist." Why are Italians so afraid of asking questions? "If we sell this apartment I wouldn't want to buy something else in Venice," he says. "I'd want to really move, to move someplace totally different, away from here. Moving into Venice is not the solution," he tells me.

Since I'm not sure what the problem is, I am also unsure that Venice is the solution. He doesn't want to talk about it anymore because he knows if I understand what he really wants to do, I might just agree and then where would he be?

One thing seems clear. We can no longer live in the work site, and in late February we move to the hotel next door. The hotel closes officially from Christmas through Easter, but since two staff persons stay to keep an eye on things, the owners agree to rent us a bedroom and bath. We'll have access to a pretty country-French-furnished sitting room with an old ceramic woodstove and a small dining room with a black marble fireplace. Our room will be heated, but the corridors and sitting and dining rooms will not. Because of insurance stipulations, we will not have kitchen privileges, as the two caretakers do. A hotel kitchen, equipped, spacious, sparkling, down the hall, and I'm not allowed to use it! Or is it that they are perfectly agreeable to my using it, but are obliged to tell me not to use it?

We bring only two suitcases of clothes, some books, and the Georgian candlestick that has gone where I've gone since I was fifteen. When we need anything else, we just go next door. Our bedroom is small and square with a very high ceiling. Flemish tapestries cover two walls, pink Murano sconces flank a large mirror, and pink moiré covers the bed and drapes the long window. There are good rugs, a heavy, dark wood armoire, a sleigh bed, pretty side tables. A burgundy velvet sofa faces the garden.

The solution to the kitchen problem is through the caretakers. They can use it, and so, if I use it with them, I will be only *smudging* the rules. I am beginning to think like an Italian. The first night I bring back things to cook from the Rialto and ask Marco, one of the caretakers, if he and his colleague would like to join us round our little black fireplace about nine. I tell him I'm braising porcini in sage cream and Moscato, that I'll grill chestnut polenta with Fontina, that there are pears and walnuts and more Moscato for afterward. Smiling, he asks how I'm going to braise the porcini over the wood fire, knowing already I'm headed straight for the kitchen. I invite him to prep with me and Fernando joins us and then Gilberto comes in, finished with his painting session in the reception rooms, and soon we are all mincing and whisking and drinking Prosecco. That evening, and several evenings each week thereafter, until the proprietors come home, Marco, Gilberto, Fernando, and I keep good company round the little black fireplace in the small hotel.

Gilberto is an extrordinary cook, and when he takes a turn at

the burners, he roasts ducks and pheasant and guinea hens, stirs up
thick wintry concoctions of lentils and potatoes and cabbages. One
evening he announces we will have only dessert. He makes *kaiser-
schmarren,* delicate crèpe-like confections cut into ribbons and
swathed in wild blueberry jam. He passes a bowl of thick cream and
a bottle of iced plum eau-de-vie purloined from the hotel's private larder, and when we finish every jot, I am grateful I don't have
to climb over thirteen bridges and ride over the waters to get to
our bed. When no one cooks, we roast whole heads of garlic and
small purple onions over the fire, charring them until they collapse,
sprutzing them with good balsamic vinegar, feasting on them with
fresh white cheese, trenchers of crusty bread, and good red wine.
We live for nearly nine months in the hotel, at first like voluptuous
stowaways, then as proper guests, sitting at table with the others,
and, once in a while, exchanging mysterious smiles with Gilberto
and Marco.

I walk over to our apartment each day, but the workers are almost
never there. I'm learning another fact that affects the Italian work
ethic. The working-class Italian, the average small businessman,
wants less from his life—from his earning life—than do many
other Europeans in similar situations. What a working-class Italian
can't do without he usually already has. He wants a comfortable
place to live—whether rented or owned makes little difference to
him. He wants an automobile or a truck or both, but they will be
modest. He wants to take his family to Sunday lunch, up to the
mountains for a week in February, and down to the sea for two

weeks in August. He wants to offer a good *grappina* from the Friuli to his colleagues when it's his turn on Friday afternoon. He'd rather have money in the bank than in his wallet because he'd never spend it anyway. What he needs costs relatively little, so why should he work longer or harder to get more when he thinks himself already well-off enough?

The Italian knows that speed—say, the fitting in of another appointment or hurrying to finish something he can finish tomorrow —will give him not more satisfaction but less, if such preposterous acts interfere with his rituals. An espresso and a chat with friends will always come before the installation of your baseboard. And he knows that because you are such a lovely person, you would applaud his sense of values. When he watches a soccer match rather than work on your estimate, he knows you'll have expected him to do just that. If he uses your down payment to clear a debt rather than buy materials for your project, he is only practicing a sort of triage, the addressing of the severest need first. In the end this will serve you, as it has his customers before you and will serve those after you. Italians have learned about patience more than almost anyone else. They know that, in the end, a few months, a few years, one way or the other, will not cast long shadows over your well-being nor enlarge it. The Italian understands wrinkles in time.

And then there's the whole idea of service, which, in Italy, has never quite caught on. Here a customer base is often generations old, and, for better or worse, its numbers will rise and fall only with the birth and death rates. In Italy "cutting edge" refers to one's knives, good and sharp enough to carve up a *salame* thin as paper. There was enough innovation during the Renaissance to last another thousand years or so. Ancestral inventiveness suffices here, and few feel the need to improve on it. Who could even think to improve the wheel or a straw broom or the lead plumb that tests the straightness of a wall? Besides, if something goes amiss, the Italian can look to heaven and curse his entire lineage for thwarting him. There is always destiny to blame for any red marks that an evil accountant might enter on one's annual report. Anyway *nonna,* grandmother, and everyone else has more sympathy for a whiff of failure than for the smell of new money. Except in sports, the greater sympathy in Italy is reserved for the vanquished. The celebrity Fantozzi has long been the essential, irresistible, benign bungler in Italian film. His is the preferred identity of the working-class Italian male, including even some bankers.

Ambition is an illness in Italy, and no one wants to catch it. At least, no one wants you to know that he has caught it. If the saints and angels had desired him to be rich, rich he would be by now, he tells you. Hence workers in Italy are not less reliable, less efficient, or more cunning than workers are anywhere else. They are, instead, *Italian* workers, functioning according to a perfectly acceptable *Italian* rhythm and attitude. It is we outsiders who refuse to accept this. When an Italian rolls his eyes in mock horror at another Italian's casual approach to a day's work, there is also a sort of pride in his look that says, "Some things, thank God, will never change."

Fernando is delighted with the nightly recountings of my newly burnished takes on his countrymen, and he tells his own set of stories about the inner workings of the Italian banking system and its splendidly played farces. He laughs, yet a wisp of rancor lingers when he's quiet. I don't ask him about it, since he seems only tentatively at peace with his work-in-progress crises.

We have chosen large black and white marble tiles to cover the walls and the floor. Fernando wants them laid straight, while I think it might be interesting to place some of them on the diagonal. I sketch, and he crumples my paper and says the effect will be too contemporary. I drag him to the Accademia and Correr to illustrate how time-worn and classic black and white on the diagonal is, and he says okay. But he won't give in on the new washing machine, which he desires to be positioned exactly where the old one sat, thus carrying on the tradition of colliding with it each time we open the door. I want one of those wonders of Milanese design, a washer slim as a suitcase that lives inside a handsome cabinet. He says these machines only wash two pairs of socks at a time, that their cycles last three hours, that they are wholly impractical. I want to talk about form over function, but he says I can just drape the big machine the way I drape everything else, and so it's the big machine that we order.

I am reading a biography of Aldo Moro, the Italian prime minister who, in the sixties and into the seventies, preached, among other things, a "historic compromise" between the church and the communists. He called for a *coincidenza* of the virtues of authority and reform, what he termed "converging parallels." How sublimely Italian, at once civilized and yet socially and mathematically impossible. Each faction rolls straight ahead, alongside the other faction, and both talk across the void between them about their impending coexistence, all the while knowing it will never be. Just as in a marriage.

I ogle and fondle bolts of fabric all over Venice, but, like all the good Lidensi, I must content myself with choices from the goods stacked up in the garage next to the laboratory of Tappezzeria Giuseppe Mattesco in Via Dandolo. The entire inventory seems to be white, off-white, creamy white, pale yellow, or mint green sheer cottons and polished cottons, though there are a few flowered chintzes in shades of lilac and red and pink and an occasional maverick bolt of tapestry. Since we have only a few windows with which to work and three pieces of furniture that need slipcovering, I want some opulent satin and velvet stripe, cinnamon, bronze. I want to know why I can't buy fabric elsewhere from which Signor Mattesco can make our drapes and slipcovers, and Fernando tells me it's because, years ago, Mattesco bought out an overstocked mill up in the Treviso, hundreds and hundreds of bolts of the same fabrics, and ever since, he has been measuring and cutting and stitching up the same bargain-priced drapes and slipcovers for everyone on the island. He says working with Mattesco on Mattesco's terms is a sort of local ordinance.

I think this is a fantastic story but it turns out to be almost true, and so I feel less terrible about never having been invited into any of my neighbor's houses. Now I know in all of them flutter the same white batiste curtains bordered in little wine-colored balls. At least that's what Mattesco tries to push off on me. I dig about in his garage for days until I find a cache of ivory brocade. It is heavy and lush and smells profoundly of mold. He is so happy to get rid of the forgotten stuff he says two days in the sun will cure it, and it does, nearly, or enough so that we can use it.

Signora Mattesco is the seamstress. She has white skin and white hair and wears a pristine white smock as she sits at her machine in a sea of white cloth. She looks like an angel and seems confused, sad even, about my not wanting the border of little wine-colored balls.

There is a bottega in San Lio where a father and son pound and carve, twisting thin sheets of metal into chandeliers, lamps, and candlesticks, rubbing the beauties with woolen cloth dipped in gold paint. We've been watching them at work in their window, stopping in to visit and chat once or twice each week for months before we even begin to explore what we might like to have them make for us. They and we are happy for one another's company, and all of us know there is no hurry about deciding anything. Venetians like to stretch certain encounters out as thin as a wasp's wing, to unroll them *pian, piano,* ever so slowly. Why scurry, why settle something before it needs to be settled? If enough time passes between the set-tling and the finishing, one might find one's self not needing what it was one settled on and someone else finally finished. And anyway, where is the joy in endings? I swear I am beginning to understand Venetians. I continue to think about Rapunzel and the Italian truth that without suffering and drama nothing is worth having or doing. Without the rubble and the screaming and Fernando's dead-bird eyes, I would have only a bathroom rather than a black-and-white marble-walled and -floored room, where I will take candlelit baths with a stranger.

The Biblioteca Marciana, the Venetian National Library, is an-other room in my house. A room that is, gratefully, not under con-struction. The library is located inside a sixteenth-century palazzo designed by Jacopo Sansovino and was constructed to house the Greek and Latin collections bequeathed to Venice by Cardinal Bessariono of Trebisond. Sitting square on the edges of the stone-flagged Molo and the Piazzetta, it looks toward the Doge's Palace and Basilica San Marco. The library's spare, severe Ionic and Doric columns are neighbors across the Piazzetta with pink and white Gothic arcades and the smoky glitter of Byzantium, all of them behaving nicely together in a sort of architectural cordiality at the entrance to the earth's most beautiful piazza.

I have spent more hours inside the dank solemn space of the library than anywhere else in Venice besides my own bed in our apartment or my rented one at the hotel next door. I'm determined to learn to read better and better in Italian. I've come to know the stacks and files, where certain manuscripts and collections are shelved, and even what's behind some of the funny little doors. Free to wander about its three-quarters of a million volumes, I have come to know the particular and merciless cold that saturates its spaces in autumn and winter and to love its smells of damp paper, dust, and old stories. I know which sofa sags less than the others, which lamps actually have bulbs, which writing table gets the warmth of a space heater, and who among my companions reads aloud, who sleeps, who snores. I read-stumble-read history and apocrypha, chronicles and biographies and memoirs in my new language, often in an archaic form of my new language. Librarians, Fernando, dictionaries, my own curiosity, the will to imagine I could understand something of the ancient consciousness of Venice and the Venetians are my spurs.

On Fridays I don't go to the Marciana at all. I don't write or read a word. I don't even go to market or to Do Mori. I simply walk. More peaceful now, I revel in the gifts of whole, golden mornings with no one else's claim scrawled across them. I remember the days when, if an hour stretched out all mine, I would grab it and run, gorging on its moments as I would an apronful of warm figs. Now I have the feast of hour after hour, and so I choose a neighborhood and explore it as carefully as if I'd just acquired it in a game of blackjack. I walk in the Ghetto and in Cannaregio, or I stay on the water and debark in some unusual post.

One day in the Campo Santa Maria Formosa, I stop to buy a sack of cherries and sit on the steps of the church. Legend says a bishop from Oderzo founded this church after a majestic woman with majestic breasts, *una formosa,* appeared to him and said he should build a church there and wherever else he saw a white cloud brush the earth. The good bishop built eight churches in Venice, but only this one is called after the formidable lady. I like this story. At the base of Santa Maria's baroque bell tower there is a grotesque—a medieval *scacciadiavoli,* devil chaser. The old bell and the even older grotesque are at ease together, the sacred and the profane taking the sun.

When it's too cold to stay outdoors all day, I ride out to the islands, to Mazzorbo and Burano, or to San Lazzaro to sit in the Armenian library—but I don't read. I sit there happily among old Mechitar's manuscripts and the soft padding about of the monks and I think. Sometimes I feel as though I've lived here forever. I think about what I've read, tried to read, understood, not quite understood. I think about the sadness Venice wears, that faint half-mourning that becomes her. And sometimes I see her naked, her sad mask loosed a moment and look straight into a face that's not sad at all. And I begin to understand she's done the same for me, loosed *my* sad mask, so old I wore it like skin.

In my readings I often come upon some ripple of lust, some small scrap of it, lust being a historic Venetian impulse. Sexual, sensual, and economic hungers drove la Serenissima. A place of arrivals, brief soujourns, debarkings was Venice when she was new as much as she is still. A stopping-off place like no other, the insubstantialness of Venice bewitched. A sanctuary for indulgence. In the fifteenth century more than fourteen thousand women were registered with the city governors as licensed and tax-paying courtesans. A volume was published each year, serving as a guide to the hospitality of these women. It presented short biographies, the family and social alliances, education, and training in arts and letters of each courtesan. The book assigned each one a number, so that when the king of France or an English noble, a soldier waiting his billet on the next Crusade, a mirror-maker in from Murano, a Carthaginian trafficking in pepper and nutmeg came to town and sought some feminine succor, he could send a porter round to the lady's often sumptuous address, requesting an audience with number 203, or 11,884, or 574.

Should a courtesan's business lull, she would go for an afternoon to stroll. In wide, fluttering crinolines, red-blond hair woven with gems, white unsunned skin safe under a parasol, she would troll the piazza and the *campi,* beckoning this one with a deep curtsy, another one with the quick fluttering of her fan or a half-moment's baring of her breast. A Venetian courtesan wore *zoccoli,* sandals built up on twenty-inch pedestals—stilts, really—which served to keep her frock from wet and soil while raising her up from the crowds, identifying her.

The Venetian aristocracy and the merchant class, along with the clergy, partook of the sophisticated social ministrations of these goddess spies who kept state secrets, if only for a while, and told truths, if not all of them. These women were as often the wives and daughters of the nobility as they were those of a policeman or a stonemason. Sometimes they were young women who'd been parceled off to convents by their middle-class, dowry-fearing fathers. These unwilling postulants often violated their vows by secret and not-so-secret forays into this other, this less chaste sisterhood. The convent of San Zaccaria became celebrated for its libertine nuns, for the conspirings and plots they birthed along with a bevy of illegitimate children. Under the inquisition of a bishop's council, one of these nuns is said to have offered up the defense that her service to the church was greater than her sin upon it, she, after all, having kept as many priests as she could from a slip into homosexuality.

Whatever lust now titillates the Byzantine core of a Venetian he will often reserve for travelers rather than his neighbors. There is a *locandiere,* owner-manager, of a simple *pensione* and a four-table *osteria* who hasn't tuned up his menu for thirty years. Each morning he cooks the same five or six genuine, typical Venetian dishes. The food he doesn't sell on a given day he nicely sets apart and conserves. Next day he cooks again, presenting the just-made dishes to his daily customers and the more mature rice and peas or pasta and beans or fish stew to passersby. Hence, the couple from New Zealand is eating the same type of food as are the two Venetian matrons who sit next to them. It's just that the New Zealanders' food is seasoned with two or three days' worth of patina for which the *locandiere* is wont to charge them thirty percent more than he does the ladies from *Sant'Angelo* whom he will see again the next day. He knows he'll never see those New Zealanders again and isn't Venice, herself, enough to content them? What do they know from pasta and beans, anyway? A merchant of Venice often sees himself separate from his product, be it fish or glass or hotel rooms. He is neither diminished nor enhanced by his own slipperiness, by his asking vulgar fistfuls of lire for yesterday's fish, slipperiness being another form of masquerade and masquerade being his birthright. The prostitute nun, the ermine-cloaked beggar, the doge who signed a pact on the day of his coronation that left him virtually powerless, these particularly Venetian forms of minor key harmony have given way to less reckless expressions of "coexistence," sometimes in the form of "pot A and pot B" of pasta and beans.

# 15

# The Return of Mr. Quicksilver

We are trying to find the right place to breakfast on the rocks along the dam in Alberoni early one Saturday in July. Stepping over and around poles and buckets and lanterns and armies of stray cats that besiege the fishermen, Fernando opens quietly, "You know that idea about selling the apartment? I think we should do it. It's going to be beautiful when it's finished, and Gambara says our investment in the renovation will permit an interesting gain for us." Gambara is the real estate agent in the Rialto whom we finally went to see and who has come several times to look at the work-in-progress. Our consulting with Gambara was an exercise in collecting intelligence, we'd agreed, impressions and numbers to stash away for someday. Is it someday already? Fernando thinks me a revolutionary, but it's he who is the anarchist.

"When do you decide these things? Am I always across the water when these holy flashes strike you?" I ask. All I wanted was to drink this cup of cappuccino and eat this apricot pastry while sitting on a rock in the sunshine. "How *sure* are you about wanting this?" I ask him.

"*Sicurissimo.* Absolutely sure," he says, as though it's steel.

"Have you thought about where you'd like to look for another house?" I try.

"Not exactly," he says.

"I guess we'll have to look in the quarters we can afford and hope we can find something we like. Probably Cannaregio or Castello, don't you think?" I ask him as though it's already steel with me, too.

"Remember when I told you if we sell our place I'd want to move somewhere totally different?"

"Sure I remember. Venice *is* totally different from the Lido, and we'll find a house with a little garden so you can have roses, and we'll have big windows with lots of light and some wonderful view, rather than having to look out at Albani's satellite dish and the troll's decrepit Fiat, and we can walk everywhere without having to be on the water half our lives. Believe me, Venice will be totally different." I say all this very quickly, as though my speaking will prevent him from speaking, because I don't want to hear what I think he is going to say next.

"I'm leaving the bank."

It's worse than what I thought he was going to say. Or is it better? No, it's worse.

"I don't know how much time we have before one of us dies or gets terribly sick or something, but I want to spend all of it together. I want to be where you are. I just don't have another ten or twelve or fifteen years in me to give to this job." He's very still now.

"What would you like to do?" I ask.

"Something together. So far, that's all I know," he says.

"You don't want to transfer to another bank, then?" I ask.

"Another bank? Why? I'm not looking for another version of this life. What would be the point of changing banks? One bank is just like another bank. I want to be with you. It's not as though I'll leave tomorrow. I'll wait until we arrange things so that we won't be hurt by my leaving. But please understand me when I tell you *I am* going to leave," he says.

"But isn't selling the house the last thing we do rather than the first? I mean, if we sell the house, where do we go?" I want to know.

"It will take years to sell the apartment. Gambara says the market is very slow. You know everything moves *pian, piano* here," he says like balm. Everything except you, I think. My vision is fading and my heart is thrashing, climbing up into my throat. I flash back to the apartment and back to Saint Louis. I even think back to California. Didn't I just arrive here? Isn't Venice my home?

"Why do you want to go away from Venice?" I whisper at him.

"It's less that I want to leave Venice than it is that I want to go somewhere else. Venice will always be part of us. But our life is not dependent on one place. Or one house or one job. I learned all that from you. I like this 'always being a beginner' idea, and now I want to be one," he tells me. Fernando has never really moved and I don't know if he even understands what it takes. The spiritual move, I mean. Have I made it all sound too simple? I do that. I've always cooked and smiled and curled my hair through tempests. A whistler in caves, a sparkler in the doom, I sauté red herrings. Have I, Pollyanna, inspired him to imagine us as bold children with apples and cookies and cheese tied up in a bandana, off to live in a boxcar, off to cut the opening-day ribbons on a lemonade stand?

My serenity is not built into our new smooth soon-to-be-painted-ocher walls any more than it has been built into other walls. I know we are all waterbirds, camped in stilt houses only a breeze above a coursing sea. And this thought has always excited as much as it terrified me. At this moment, though, I'm feeling only the part about the terror. I wonder how much of my serenity is swirled, if not in the walls, then into this sea and this lagoon, how much of it has seeped into this thin, rosy light, how much more of it hangs in these oriental fogs. I just don't know right now. Or do I? Can I take it all with me once again? Will the whole of Venice become another room in my house?

And there's another part to my terror, the thought of inventing the next era, some other way to live, some other thing to do. The little engine that always could. Am I a little engine that still can? And if *I* can, can *he*?

Staking out a large flat rock for us, he makes me a pillow with his sweatshirt and we sit together. I shiver in the July sun. Strangely feeble, its heat feels like new April heat, and the sea and the sky and his eyes are all the same blue. I feel feeble, too. I think of all those sinews and spines, the weeding and digging he's done to get to this point. "Good for you," I say through my shivers. Just as one can see the young face in a person who is old, right this minute I can see Fernando's old face in his still young one. I think how much more I'll love him then. I remember the four generations of women who walked over the bridge on the festival of la Salute. Young faces inside old faces. Old faces inside young ones. If we dare to really look, how much more we can see.

"There will be no pension available for twelve years," he says, as though I didn't know that. "It's only an idea," he says, which I know means, "It's the thing I want to do most in the world. Today."

We sit there on the rock without speaking. We are so tired from not speaking that we fall asleep and it's nearly noon when we wake.

We spend the afternoon and evening making fifty trips back and forth from the hotel to the work site, as though we can't be certain which of the two environments is the better place to think. Sometimes we talk, but mostly we are silent. His part of the silence tells me he's thoroughly convinced we should leave Venice. Still, I don't understand his compulsion. If I could only be sure *he* understands his compulsion. Our finding each other has affected us almost reversely. It's not as though we've come closer at all. It's that each one has jumped the river into the other one's woods. It's O. Henry. I, the wanderer, full of tears and cornmeal crumbs, have become a nestling, while he, the sleeper, has become a rolling stone. He says no. He says it's not that we've switched sides of the river, it's that we've both jumped in. And he says I'm only tired from holding up the moon for him. "Now, I feel as though the two of us are more the same one. Strains healing, edges smoothing, if you'll be patient, you'll see," he says quietly.

"Okay," I tell him. I say we will proceed deliberately, shaping things carefully, letting the fates rest while we open and close our own doors.

"Patience," we promise each other.

In the last days of September, the *operai* begin moving out their tools and equipment, bequeathing us nine months of detritus and a beautiful new apartment. We shovel and sweep and scour, and soon the little place is glowing. Mattesco comes to hang the drapes, and, piece by piece, we put things in order.

Though it is not yet officially for sale, it has become like my house in Saint Louis before, a place we are waiting to leave.

We comb through weekly journals and real-estate publications that post new business offerings and after supper we lay them out, read them to each other, tear, staple, stack, file, discard, then read, again, the ones we've saved. Fernando is convinced we should find a small hotel, a country house with a dozen rooms, a place where we can live as well as work. "But can you really see us as innkeepers?" I ask him, fondling the one newspaper that deals exclusively with restaurant opportunities.

"Yes. I absolutely can. One of us speaks English, one speaks Italian, and this is already a plus. If you can transform the apartment, think what we can do together to transform any other ruin, make it comfortable, inviting, romantic, a place travelers could come home to. I know it will be hard at first because we'll have to do everything ourselves, but we'll be together," he tells me.

I want to show him an entry I've found in the restaurant journal. I have begun to see in him some reserved but freshly piqued interest in food. He's ordering more courageously in restaurants, walking over from the bank to meet me at the Rialto some mornings so we can shop together for supper and then sitting in our little kitchen, watching what I do with the white eggplant he's chosen. He'll crane his head round my shoulder as I tip handfuls of tiny golden mushrooms into a pan, sizzling them up in sweet butter scented with sharp, wild onions one of the market farmers had dug up along the banks of the river Brenta. Fernando says the mushrooms smell like the forest where he used to walk with his grandfather. He buys a rosemary plant and tends it like a just-born baby. Still, I fear it's too soon to open discourse on the possibility of our spending the future heaving stockpots and easing our Wusthofs across oiled carborundum stone. I move in more frugally. "It would be nice if we could offer guests the option of staying to dinner, don't you think?" I say, barely sprinkling the seed.

But the stranger doesn't hear me. Deep in road dreams, he's measuring distances on his maps. First to second knuckle is one hundred kilometers. "I'll take every Friday off so we'll have four three-day weekends every month to travel."

"How can you do that?" I want to know.

"What are they going to do, fire me? We can reach almost any destination in the north in less than ten hours," he tells me, hopping and skipping his bent finger across Italy like a chess piece.

We read about a small hotel for sale in Comeglians on the sun-forsaken edges of the Friuli near the Austrian border, and we go to find it. We've agreed our territory is everything north of Rome, and so we drive three thousand feet up onto the lonely stone stretches of the Carnia, where the temperature on an August Friday at high noon registers thirty-seven degrees Fahrenheit. The first thing I notice are all the signs that say *legna da ardere,* wood to burn, along the rough, serpentine roads. I try to imagine February. We're lost, and we stop to ask the way at the tobacconist who is also the grocer, the cheesemaker, and the local grappa distiller and who at this moment is hacking a wedge from a great wheel of hard, whiffy Carnian cheese. Thrusting his javelin-like tool between our heads he says, *"Sempre diritto,* always straight." One of the few interregional commonalities among Italians is how they give directions. They agree all destinations are reached by a straight line. I already miss the sea.

There are twenty bedrooms and eight bathrooms in the stone-and-wood chalet-style hotel, a small bar to one side, and, on the other, an immense fireplace, round and low, with an unsheltered hearth—a *fogolar* in the Friulano dialect. The fire is spent, but the scent of last night's woodsmoke greets us.

The signora wants to sell because, since regional and state funding for road building slid off the docket in the late seventies, there have been no workers from Tolmezzo and Udine and Pordenone who would come to sleep in her twenty beds and sit with tumblers of grappa round the *fogolar,* who would eat ten kilos of sausages and ten more of beefsteak in an evening and a whole cauldron full of polenta that the signora had made from white cornmeal and poured out, steaming, onto a thick wooden board set close by the fire. She says she'll give me her recipe for the sauce of sheep's intestines and red wine that's delicious with polenta. Fernando asks about tourism, and she tells him that people mostly stay in and around Tolmezzo or San Daniele del Friuli, that there's nothing much to bring them into Comeglians, but that with a little patience the workers will be back. "*Vedrai.* You'll see," she says as we wave good-bye to her from the car.

We are exploring a bit in Verona, having heard about a *locanda* with eight rooms for sale in Via XX Settembre, when, over a glass of Recioto at the Bottega del Vino, a man dressed in whisky-colored suede who'd been candidly eavesdropping on our Esperanto, introduces himself. He says he's meeting some American friends for dinner and invites us to join them. Plausible in New York, this is outrageous and invasive behavior, a stab in the elegantly woven Veronese reserve. But we consider it over another glass of wine and half an hour's preamble to our life stories before gracefully refusing and exchanging business cards. When he leaves, the barman tells us our companion is a count, a gentleman farmer, a champion horseman whose estate is up in the hills of Solferino in Lombardy. We say, "How lovely," and go off to Al Calmiere to eat *pastissada,* smoked horsemeat braised in tomatoes and red wine. Back in Venice, the count has already left us a message.

We are invited to spend next weekend on his farm, and we accept. He has an eighteenth-century villa with a half dozen cottages and paddocks and barns scattered over the velvet, silken lands where the Gonzaga were once lords. The count invites us again and again. He asks us to come for a weekend of riding and hunting, to cook, if we wish, that we'll go to the markets and the cheesemakers, the winemakers, that we'll collect provisions for a four-day feast. I look to Fernando, who surprises me as well as the count with a vigorous, decisive, *"Perché no?* Why not?"

The count's guests are mostly English, with a German couple and two Scotsmen. Aproned and scrubbed, Fernando and I roll out dough for tortelli and plump them big as teacup saucers with roasted pumpkin and crushed *amaretti,* crisp almond macaroons, and slivers of *mostarda,* fruit preserved in mustard oil. We set beef to marinate in an old gray crock and drown it in Amarone; we make buckwheat polenta with braised quail and risotto the way the rice farmers once made it in the fields. Each day's lunch we seal with the heel of a Franciacorta and a thick, runny wedge of Gorgonzola, drizzled with the count's wild thyme honey.

The guests ride and eat and drink. By the third day, everyone, except the Scotsmen, leave off riding for long sleeps broken only by the call to table. The whole event is luscious. When the count offers us a home and lucrative positions, we listen, but we tell him it's our own adventure we're after and not a portion of his. These few days

seem to have empowered Fernando. He's talking about developing
knife skills, and asking about the difference between naturally cave-
aged Gorgonzola and the sham kind that's shot full of copper wires
to accelerate the formation of it's whiffy green veins. He seems
invigorated.

For three, sometimes four days of each week we race over the autostrada and curl up mountain roads and careen back down them
to skim past vineyards and groves of olives, alongside tobacco fields
and sheepfolds and sunflowers toward the next city, the next hill-
town, the next medieval village. We drive through the Tuscan hills of
Botticelli, Leonardo da Vinci, and Piero della Francesca, pink sand
slopes buttoned in black cypress, the red Siena earth just turned and
waiting, the powdery light, a watercolor landscape of mulberries,
figs, olives, and vines. If I can't look at the sea, I want to look at this.
But we don't find a house in Tuscany.

We talk with every real estate agent and tourist officer we can
find, every fruitseller, baker, and barman we meet. We stalk and
prowl and shadow those we think might inform us. We wave down
farmers from their tractors and, over the grinding of their motors,
they point us to ruins in far-off fields. And just when we're tired and
hungry enough to cry, we find some small *osteria* at the edge of an
unlit gravel path that traverses a wheat field and are fed a great
golden tangle of pasta by a lady who's been rolling it out there twice
a day for half a century.

We don't find a house, but we find a handmade sign that says,
*"Oggi cinghiale al buglione.* We follow the sign to a renovated stable
and a farmer's wife who sits us down on wooden benches while she

braises a boar's haunch with garlic and tomatoes and white wine over an olive wood fire. We eat and drink with people who have never seen Venice or Rome, who have never lived anywhere but the place where they were born. We don't find a house, but we find a mill in a chestnut grove driven by a wooden paddlewheel powered by a stream that's been roiling since the mastodons. We find grape growers who still celebrate the harvest and the crush with torchlit suppers among the vines, and olive farmers who harvest the green-purple-black almost mature fruit by hand and press it between ancient stones turned round and round by a mule. The oil is green as grass and full of tiny, stinging bubbles. It smells like roasted hazelnuts, and, when the oil is spilled out over hot wood-roasted bread and whispered with sea salt, it tastes like the only food in a perfect world.

Bruised from trekking through rains and heat and climbing crumbling stairs, we keep going, week after week, until more than a year has passed. Still, there is no small hotel, no farmhouse-to-renovate, no place to work, and no place to live. It's Christmas Eve, and we are heading back to Venice after another of our journeys when Fernando veers off the road. "How would you like to spend Christmas in Austria?" he wants to know, reaching for one of our six hundred map books.

"We can be in Salzburg by six." We're prepared enough; an overnight bag always waits in the trunk. What about our presents and the tortellini and the turkey with the walnut pesto stuffed under his skin waiting back in Venice? He says we'll have Christmas all week. At least I'm wearing new boots and my green velvet hat. He is telling me there is sure to be snow, and I'm saying, "Let's go," and when we arrive at the Weisses Rossl, a string quartet is playing "Silent Night" in front of a crèche across the way. It snows.

Fernando was right, I think, as we walk back to the hotel after midnight mass. Surely these have been journeys to find the next part of our lives, but more, they have been journeys toward the center. We have been married for two years. I try to remember life without him and it's like trying to remember an old film I thought I'd seen but perhaps never did. I ask him if he's sorry we didn't find each other when we were young, and he says he would never have recognized me when he was young. And besides, he was too old when he was young, he says.

"I feel the same way," I tell him, remembering when I, too, was so much older.

⌒

We decide to go to New York to meet up with the children, to visit friends. On the day before our departure, we walk in the Rialto and Fernando says, "Let's stop in and tell Gambara to put the apartment on the market. Maybe we have to approach the change from another direction." We sign up the apartment and go home to finish packing.

Packing and unpacking, it's all we do. We are a touring company. My secret to serene travel is to wear everything I can't afford to lose, and because it's February, this task is easy. I am layering a tweed vest over two thin cashmere sweaters over a silk shirt, a long wide suede skirt over slim leather pants when Gambara rings to say he will be coming by at eleven with a potential buyer, a Milanese named

Giancarlo Maietto who wants a beach house for his retired father. At eleven we'll be somewhere over the Tyrrhenian Sea I tell him, and he says to leave the keys with the troll and to call him the next day from New York.

But we don't call him on the next day, or on the day after that. On our third day in New York we are tucked in at Le Quercy behind plates of duck confit and potatoes that are dark gold from a fast, hot dalliance with a pint of duck fat. A bottle of Vieux Cahors is close at hand. Fernando says he feels guilty for not calling and wants to call right then, even though it's seven-thirty in the morning in Venice. I am wholly absorbed in duck thighs and wine and, through eyes half-closed, I wave him on to the telephone. My face and hands are glossy with duck fat when he returns to the table to say, "Giancarlo Maietto bought the apartment." I exchange my clean plate with his, still full of confit, and I continue to eat. "What are you doing? How can you eat when we don't have a place to live?" he whines.

"I'm living in the moment," I tell him. "I may not have a place to live, but right now I do have this duck, and before you put it up for sale I'm going to eat it. And anyway it was you who said perhaps change must come from another direction—and so it did. It's all going to be fine," says Pollyanna through lips ornamented in two purply points, a sensualist's mustache earned from deep drinking the Cahors. The return of Mr. Quicksilver. Will he always resist more than two palmy days in a row?

By the end of our first week in New York, the offer, the counter-offer, and the countered counteroffer have been proposed and accepted. Maietto will pay only a sliver less than our pitilessly high asking price. Because he knew we were not yet hard-pressed to sell the house, Gambara told Fernando to shoot for the stars, and he did. Back in Venice we meet with Gambara who tells us Maietto wants possession in sixty days, but we ask for a ninety and Maietto agrees. On the fifteenth of June we will leave. To go where, we must yet divine. We tell ourselves we must be diligent, keep looking. If we come up empty, we'll put our things in storage and rent a furnished place in Venice until we come up flush. That's what we say, but Fernando has the sighs, the angsts, and on the morning he's due back at the bank he asks if I'll take the early boat with him and walk with him to work.

We walk right past the bank as though he forgot it was there, and when we meet one of the tellers outside he throws him the keys to the safe and says, *"Arrivo subito.* I'm coming right away."

We walk out of San Bartolomeo, past the post office and over the Ponte dell'Olio, and he's not saying a word. The Princess is beautiful this morning, peeking from behind her March veils. When I ask him if he doesn't think so, too, he doesn't hear me. We stop in at Zanon for an espresso and then rush over the Ponte San Giovanni Crisostomo, as though this was the way to the bank rather than away from it. We're almost running now, along the Calle Dolfin and over another bridge into Campo Santi Apostoli, full of children screaming their way to school, and then into Campo Santa Sofia and onto Strada Nuova. He says nothing until we come up to the *vicolo* that leads out to the Ca' d'Oro landing stage. And then all he says is, "Let's go back." We ride but we don't debark at the next stop, which is the bank, so I think we're going home. Instead we get off at Santa Maria del Giglio, and he says, "Let's go into the Gritti for coffee," as though it's our habit to take a ten-thousand-lira espresso in Venice's most plush hotel.

He doesn't sit with me at the little table in the bar but plunks down a fresh package of cigarettes and his lighter and asks the waiter to bring a cognac. "Only one, sir?" asks the barman.

"Yes. Only one," he says, still standing. To me he says softly, "Smoke these, drink this, and wait for me right here." He has perhaps forgotten I don't smoke and that I like my cognac after dinner rather than at nine-thirty in the morning! He's gone in a flash. But where? Has he gone to call Gambara and kill off the sale? Could he even do that if he'd wanted to?

Half an hour, perhaps thirty-five minutes pass, and he reappears. He is dazed and looks as though he's been crying. *"Ho fatto.* I did it. I walked over to Via XXII Marzo to the main office and climbed the stairs up to the director's office, and I walked in and I sat down and I told him I was leaving," he says, tracing his every move to assure himself he'd really made each one of them. Always in control of his *bella figura,* now he is unselfconscious in this Lilliputian space among the barmen and the concierge, three men drinking beer and a woman puffing on a very large cigar. He proceeds with his story. "And do you know what Signor d'Angelantonio said to me? He said, 'Do you want to write your letter here, now, or bring it to me tomorrow? As you wish.' *'As you wish,'* was all he had to say to me after twenty-six years. Well, I did as I wished," he says. He tells me he sat down in front of a manual Olivetti and pecked out his salvo, that he tore it from the rollers and folded it in three and asked for an envelope, which he addressed to d'Angelantonio, who still stood a yard away behind a desk.

I have learned these tempests of his are not tempests at all but only the last quick darts of lightning that come after long, seething reflection. Fernando's passages are nearly always silent and nearly always private. I understand this, and still he staggers me. I reach for the untouched cognac and try to begin lining things up in my mind. I think the story goes something like this. I come to Venice and meet a stranger who works in a bank and lives on the beach. The stranger falls in love with me and comes to Saint Louis to ask me to marry him, to ask me to leave my house and my work and come to live happily ever after with him on the fringes of a little island in the Adriatic Sea. I, too, fall in love and I say *I will,* and so I do. The stranger who is now my husband decides he no longer wishes to live on the fringes of a little island in the Adriatic Sea nor work in a bank, and so now neither he nor I have a house or work and we are beginning at the beginning. Incredibly, I am at ease with all of this. It's only the whiplash way in which he moves that stings. What happened to patience? Then again there has been not one prudent act in this story.

I drink a ten o'clock cognac, and I cry and laugh. It's the old terror-and-joy two-punch, once again. Anyway, what does it matter that we are doing everything backward and sideways? In ten minutes I'll have found my wind. Still I ask him, "Why today and why without our having talked about it?"

"*Sono fatto così.* This is the way I am," he says. A clean self-acquittal, unambiguous, selfish I think. Fernando is Venetian, a son of the Princess. And on both their faces folly and courage look the same, bleeding into this morning's muslin light.

# 16

# Ten Red Tickets

*B*ack at the apartment, which in eighty-one days will belong to this man called Maietto, we take our portfolio
and a pot of tea to the bed that will probably always be
ours. We tally up our resources for the hundredth time, but nothing changes. The severance payment from the bank, the proceeds
from the house, what's left of our savings, a few other assets, and,
before the tea is cold, our financial meeting is finished and we lie
there feeling, in a way, excited but more than anything else, *little*.
Not "little" as in "diminished" or "fragile" but as in "new." We begin
sifting through possibilities that might permit our economic in-
dependence. We have illusions of neither ease nor grandeur ahead.
We are, indeed, going off to launch a lemonade stand, but we both
know I'll drape it in old damask and pour the lemonade into thin,
crystal goblets.

We're running out of time. Ruthlesslessly, we narrow our geography to a patch of southern Tuscany. Sunday morning rain falls in
leaden sheets, the windshield wipers beat a dirge. We head toward
Chianciano, Sarteano, Cetona, then up a mountain road where we've
never been. We wind up and up to the crest full of pine and oak
woods. It's beautiful. "Where are we going?" Fernando asks and I tell
him the map promises the tiny village of San Casciano dei Bagni.

"Roman baths. Thermal waters to cure problems of the eye. Medieval towers. Population, 200." I read the facts in a fake, cheery voice. The descent is less sinuous until it becomes more so, until the last, brusque veer to the left and then—just as it's been for one or the other or both of us at other moments in this life of ours together—nothing is the same. The road ends and we stop the car.

Straight ahead, up a hill, we see the village towers, looming out of the mist. It seems a place conjured. Miniature, heaped-up stone houses, red Tuscan roofs polished by the rain, clouds wrapping it, concealing it, before the wind blows it clean and we see it's real. Leaving the car below, we walk up the slope to the village. A man with a single wide, sharp tooth and a navy beret sits in the hush of the piazza's only bar, still as furniture. We tiptoe up to him and begin a gentle interrogation.

He tells us two families own most everything in and around the town. These are the ancestors of warring factions, medieval enemies of the blood, and we can be certain neither one of them will sell even an olive tree. He says they survive by minimally remodeling one property at a time and then renting it long-term to artists, writers, actors, and anyone else prepared to pay a high price for Tuscan solitude.

He seems to know everything. He is the sacristan of San Leonardo, on his way, now, to lead a funeral march from the church down to the cemetary. *"Infarto.* Heart attack," he tell us. "Valerio was standing right where you're standing only yesterday, and after we took our morning *grappina* together he went home and he died, *poveraccio,* poor man. Only eighty-six he was." He says we can walk along with the mourners if we'd like, that it might be a good way to get to know people, but we decline.

In parting, he urges us to chat with the matriarch of one of the
dominant families. There's work being done on one of her proper-
ties, *un podere,* a farmhouse, on the road to Celle sul Rigo, a few
yards outside the village. "She's eighty-nine and ferocious," he warns.
When we knock on her door, she shrieks down from the third floor
that she wants nothing to do with any witnesses of Jehovah. We tell
her we're only Venetians looking for a house. All blue hair and
cheekbones, she is hesitant, but we lure her into parting with the
truth that there is reconstruction in progress on one of her farm-
houses. Yes, we can see it, but not today. No, it is not for sale. She
has yet to decide on the rent, and do we know how many people
from Rome have been waiting for how many years to rent a house in
this area? We say that all we know is that this a beautiful village, that
we'd like to live here. Come back next week, she says. We hike up
the road to the house, circling it again and again, searching for reasons not to fight for it. We can't find one.

Made of crudely cut stone, taller than it is wide, it's a sober place
whose spare garden spills out and down to a meadow and a sheep-
fold and then down further onto the lane that twists back up to the
village. We stand at the edge of the garden under a vault of still-
weeping Tuscan sky. There is no epiphany, no great jubilation. We
do not see stars at noon in the rain. But softly entranced we are, as
if kissed by a witch with half her powers. We look to the village and
the chain of yellow and green valleys pleated and tucked around and
beyond it, to the Cassia, the ancient road to Rome. It is a humble
estate, and, perhaps, a good place for us to be.

There's a second-story window that has been left open just a
crack, so I step from the little porch up onto some crude scaffolding,

raise the window higher and catapult myself into a bathroom, onto a floor of brutally ugly, just-laid, puce-colored tile. The stranger follows me inside and, wandering through it, we tell each other it feels like home.

＿

All the floating pieces drop into place. The apartment is really sold. Fernando has really retired from the bank. The blue-haired matriarch agreed to a two-year lease, and we really are going to live in a tiny Tuscan village. Though we are free to move in during the first days of May, we decide to pack leisurely and depart Venice on June 15. With our long dramas quieted, we want simply *to be* in Venice and then to part with her peacefully.

We perform a ceremony of the dead for the alarm clock, but still Fernando wakes each morning precisely half an hour before sunrise. His groans of disbelief wake me, and soon we're both on our feet. I pull an Aereonautica Militare sweatshirt over one of Victoria's oldest Secrets, slip into Wellies. Fernando wears Ray-Bans even in the dark, and we stumble across the road to watch the sea and the sky light up. In our folkloric costumes we are Maggion's first customers, and we take our paper tray of warm apricot *cornetti* and the old Bialetti coffee maker, steaming and sputtering, back to bed. Sometimes we doze a bit, but usually we dress and head down to the boats.

Fernando carries a small yellow portfolio everywhere, filled with articles on olive farming and his designs for the bread oven that he'll build from the ruins of an outdoor fireplace in the garden in Tuscany. He has planted in little plastic pots twelve eight-inch-high olive trees that he plans to transplant down the western slope of the gar-

den. He's calculating that his first harvest will happen, if all goes rea-
sonably well, in twenty-five years and will yield a cup and a third of
oil. He packs one box or carton or suitcase each day with the hand-
wringing glee of a boy off to summer camp.

"I'm so exciting," he says fifty times a day in his weird English. I
look at him sometimes and wonder how he'll fare out there on dry
land behind the lemonade stand rather than in a palazzo sitting above
the lagoon, behind a marble-topped desk.

"You know, we're likely going to be poor, at least for a while," I
tell him.

"We're already poor," he reminds me. "Like any under-capitalized
business, like any under-capitalized life, we'll have to be patient. Big
way. Small way. Hard. Not so hard. If we can't make one thing work,
we'll make another thing work."

On our last Saturday morning he says, "Show me a part of Venice
you think I've never seen." So we ride the vaporetto to the Zattere.
Even though we've already had two breakfasts, I pull him into Nico
and order three hazelnut gelatos drowned in espresso. "Three, why
three?" he wants to know. I just take the extra cup and the extra little
wooden spoon and tell him to follow me. We walk the few yards
to the Squero San Trovaso, the oldest workshop in all the city, where
gondolas are still built and repaired. I introduce my husband to Fed-
erico Tramontin, a third-generation gondola builder, who is sanding
the prow of a new boat with two hands, his arms stretched out taut.
He tells Fernando he's using jeweler's sandpaper, fine enough to
smooth gold. He knows I already know this. I hand him his gelato
and Fernando and I sit on a plank off to the side, each one of us stirring and sipping at the luscious potion. We say a word or two about

the weather and then another word or two about what a pleasure it's been to have spent this time together. I'm still in the lead as I draw Fernando up to a tiny storefront travel agency, in whose grimy window there is posted a hand-wrought sign, an old invitation from Yeats.

> Come away, O human child!
> To the waters and the wild
> With a faery, hand in hand,
> For the world's more full of weeping than you can understand.

I translate the words for Fernando and tell him that when I came upon this sign during my first few weeks in Venice, I had thought the poem was for him, that *he* was the lost child; now, though, I sometimes think it's *me* who is a bit lost. But which one of us is not? Which one of us does not long to be hand in hand with a faery who knows more than we do about this sad world? That's marriage, taking turns being the lost child, being the faery.

The shops are just opening when we come, on another morning, to walk in the Strada Nuova. Everything echoes here. A man whistles while he sweeps outside his shop, where he sells rubber boots and fishing gear, and a man across the way is polishing smooth-skinned violet eggplants and laying them in a wooden box and he whistles the same song. They are a coincidental duet. Water purling up against the *fondamenta,* the embankment; bells, foghorns, feet shuffling up a bridge, down a bridge. Everything resonates. Sometimes I think Venice has no present, that she is made all of memories, the old ones and those *aldilà,* beyond. New memories, old memories are the same in Venice. Here there are only encores of a diaphanous *pas de deux. Veni etiam,* come back again. A Latin invitation from which, some say, Venice was named. Even the name is a reflection. Which image is the real image? The one reflected? The one reflecting? I touch Fernando's face as I look at it, mirrored, shimmering in the canal.

"Who do you think we'll be when we're old?" I ask him.

"Well, by some standards, we *are* old so I guess we'll be as we are right now. But the truth is I'm not sure we'll have time to really get old, what with one beginning and another," he says.

"Do you think you'll miss Venice very much?" I ask him.

"I'm not sure, but whenever we miss being here, we'll just come back to visit," he says.

"I want to come back every year for the Festa del Redentore," I tell him.

Palladio built the church of the Redeemer, in 1575, on the island of Guidecca, across from San Marco, in thanksgiving for the ending of yet another long siege of the plague. And each year since, the Venetians have rejoiced with their own sacred hallelujah of sails and lights and water. On the prescribed afternoon in July, every Venetian with a boat converges in the Bacino San Marco at the mouth of the Guidecca Canal, and the festival begins. The boats are draped in flowers and flags and are so dense in the water, one can pass a glass of wine to one sitting in the boat next door. One throws a sweater to a friend, a box of matches to another. And if the boats are small enough, boards or an old door can be balanced between them, an impromtu table for *aperitivi* together.

The feast of the Redentore is a reunion, when the Venetians celebrate themselves. They are saying, *"Siamo Veneziani.* We are Venetians. Look at us. See how we've survived. Shepherds and farmers, we survived to become fishermen and sailors who built up lives where there was no land. We've survived Goths and Longobards, Tartars and Persians and Turks. Pests and emperors and popes, we've survived them, too. And, we are still here."

Everything is ritual on the night of the Redeemer. As the sun sets, candles are lit on the prows, makeshift tables are set, and supper is served: pots full of pasta and beans tied up in linen towels and braised lagoon duck stuffed with sausages, fried sardines and sole in *saor.* Demijohns of Incrocio Manzoni and Malbec empty at an alarming pace; watermelon awaits midnight. It is the festival when one sees that figments and chimera are real; when fireworks are as normal as stars, their light another side of the moon. Everyone stays on the water until, at two or so, like a tired, victorious flotilla, the great white sails and the small patched ones inhale the soft wet breeze and move, to the sound of mandolins, slowly, slowly up-lagoon toward the Lido to watch the Redeemer's sunrise.

"It's my festival, too," I tell Fernando. "I'm Venetian as much as if I were born here. I'm Venetian, Fernando. I'm more Venetian than you," I say.

We had agreed that there would be no weeping farewell to Venice, but as I pull the sticky brown tape tight across the flaps of another box, I wonder how Fernando can be leaving so cavalierly. I don't want to leave her. Usually so good at tucking and rolling the ending of one thing into the beginning of the next, I just can't seem to do that now. I remember the very first time I left Venice. That was long before my life with the stranger. So many years have passed since then. I had stayed just two weeks that first visit and, already smitten, it was sad leaving her. Of course it was raining.

*The early mist is soft and warm on my face. The gilded putti I'd bought
for my children from Gianni Cavalier and wrapped in a dozen folds of
La Nuova Venezia are safe in a sack hung from my wrist. I tug the still-
damnable black suitcase back over the stones and stairs. My heels, clicking
more confidently than when I had first arrived, are the only sounds in the
predawn of the Sottoportego de le Acque. Though it is a longer walk than it
would have been to the Rialto, I want to take the boat from San Zaccaria, to
be in the piazza once more. Marooned it seems, a tenantless village in a
pewter sea. It is so beautiful. I walk across the Piazzetta, past the bell tower,
out between the columns of San Teodoro and the lion of San Marco. Just as
I turn left toward the pontile, la Marangona rings six long woeful bells. I
feel the sound in my chest as much as in my ears and I turn to look back a
moment, wondering what it might mean when the solemn old thing rings out
one's departure rather than one's arrival.*

*It's hard to tell tears from rain as I turn toward the boat. I ride Piazzale
Roma with only the railway workers for company. Certain that I am in flight
from some great sadness, some ending or spurning, they offer me a collective,
wordless sympathy. Less than an hour has passed, and I'm already missing
Fiorella and my funny little room on the second floor of her pensione. She
has packed panini: small thickly buttered breads laid with the thin, crisp
veal cutlets she had fried the evening before. I eat one of the sandwiches
every hour or so, making them last through the short flight from Venice to
Milan and then through two deplanings and reboardings, nearly all the way
home. . . .*

It's not as though we're never coming back, Fernando assures me.
When the last day arrives, we go to down to the sea and watch the
sunrise and take our *cornetti* back to bed, which is a mattress on the
floor now that all the furniture is on its way to Tuscany. We ride

over the waters and walk as we have always done and stop in at Do Mori, then on to tea in the far corner of Harry's Bar. We talk about all the things we have to do in San Casciano. We go back home to rest, to bathe one last time in the black-and-white marble bathroom. As we dress we say we'll have supper not in a place where we always go but at Conte Pescaor, a shack behind Campo San Zulian. We want a feast of Adriatic fish, and the Venetian boy I married thinks it's the last best seafood restaurant in Venice. On its dusty, screened verandah with its necklace of plastic lights we drink an icy Cartizze with a *frittura mixta,* a mixed fry of sea fish. We eat baked mussels and sauteed scallops and eel roasted with bay leaves. The waiter uncorks a '90 Recioto de Capitelli for us, and, because someone nearby is eating roasted razor clams, we do too, and then fried dog fish and just a taste of baked sea bass and fried red snapper. It's ten minutes before one in the morning when we say *buona notte* to the sleepy waiters. We walk slowly out into San Marco.

After midnight the boats run only at ninety-minute intervals. We have time. I sit side-saddle on the back of the pink marble lion in the Piazzetta. "We're going to change more than she will," I tell him. "When we return, even if we return next week, nothing will feel as it feels right now. I've been here more than a thousand days." A thousand days. A minute. A flash. Just like life I think. I hear her whisper: *Take my hand and grow young with me; don't rush; be a beginner; weave pearls in your hair; grow potatoes; light the candles; keep the fire; dare to love someone; tell yourself the truth; stay inside the rapture.* He helps me down from my saddle. It's time to go. I don't want to go. I feel as I did when I was seven or eight on a string of August evenings spent at the carnival with Uncle Charlie. He would always place ten red tickets in my open hand and help me up onto the black horse with the silver spots. And every time the music slowed and sounded crushed and my horse stood still, I'd tear off another ticket as if I was tearing off a piece of my heart and offer it up to the collector man. I'd hold my breath, and finally we'd be off again, round and round and round.

I always used my ten tickets in a row. Up there on the black horse with the silver spots I was a brave rider, galloping hard and fast, leaping over water and through dark forests, on my way to the house with the golden windows. I knew they'd be waiting for me there. I just knew they'd be there at the door and they'd take me inside and there'd be a fire and candles and warm bread and good soup and we'd eat together and we'd laugh. They would take me upstairs to my very own bed and tuck me tightly between the soft covers; they'd kiss me a million times and sing to me till I fell asleep, all the while saying they'd always loved me, always would. But ten tickets were never enough to reach the house with the golden windows. Ten red tickets. A thousand days. "Time to go," Uncle Charlie would say, helping me down.

"Time to go," says Fernando. I want to cry out to her, but no sound comes. I want to say, *I love you, tattered, wicked Princess. I love you. Moody old Byzantine mum in resewn skirts, I love you. Pearly muse rouged in cinnamon, how I love you.* My husband, who, a thousand days ago was a stranger, hears my silence. And he tells me, "She loves you, too. Always has. Always will."

# Food for a Stranger

*Porri Gratinati*

# A Gratin of Leeks

When I served this dish to the stranger in Saint Louis at our very first supper together, he told me right away that he didn't like leeks. I fibbed and called them scallions, and he left me with a dish so clean I hardly had to wash it. Later, when I sheepishly confessed I'd served him leeks, he waited months to forgive me. But now he searches out leeks in the market, buying armloads of them, so we can try to make enough of this lovely stuff to satisfy us both.

Truth is, the dish is so simple I'm hard put to write a recipe for it. It can be made with any one or any combination of these members of the lily family: leeks, shallots, onions. You can bake the mixture in individual dishes and serve them, all crusty on top and creamy underneath, as an opener. But my favorite way to eat *porri gratinati* is to heave a great big spoonful straight from my old, oval gratin dish onto a warm plate and lay just-grilled beef or pork on top so the meat's juices seep into and flavor the gratin, each component exalting the other.

> **About 12 medium-to-large leeks (approximately 3 pounds), green parts trimmed off, white part split, thoroughly rinsed, and sliced thinly into rounds (or 2 pounds of onions or scallions—try a mixture of sweet onions such as Vidalia, Walla Walla, or Texas Sweet with some big, strongly flavored yellow Spanish varieties).**
> **2 cups mascarpone**
> **1 teaspoon just-grated nutmeg**
> **1 teaspoon just-cracked pepper**
> **1½ teaspoons fine sea salt**
> **½ cup grappa or vodka**
> **⅔ cup grated Parmesan cheese**
> **1 tablespoon unsalted butter**

Place the prepped leeks into a large mixing bowl; in a smaller bowl combine all the remaining ingredients except the Parmesan and the butter, and mix well. Scrape the mascarpone mixture into the bowl with the leeks and, using two forks, evenly coat the leeks with the mixture. Spoon the leeks into a buttered oval oven dish 12 to 14 inches long, spreading the mixture evenly, or into six individual buttered oval dishes. Scatter the Parmesan over all, and bake at 400 degrees for 30 minutes or until a deep golden crust forms; 10 minutes less for smaller gratins.

*Yield:* 6 Servings

*Tagliatelle con Salsa di Noci Arrostite*

# Fresh Pasta with Roasted Walnut Sauce

*A*nother dish from our first evening together in Saint Louis. With this one, Fernando needed no coaxing. In fact, when he had finished he asked if he might have *"un altra goccia di salsa,* another drop of sauce." I set a little dish of it before him, and he proceeded to spread it on crusts of bread, eating the little tidbits between sips of red wine. I tried it that way, too, and ever since, we always make extra sauce, keeping it on hand for other uses. See suggestions below.

**THE PASTA**
Cook a pound of fresh tagliatelle, fettucine, or other "ribbon" pasta in abundant, sea-salted boiling water to the al dente stage, drain, and toss with 1½ cups of the following sauce. If fresh pasta is not available, substitute dried artisinal pasta.

**THE SAUCE** *(Makes about 2 cups)*
   **18 ounces shelled walnuts, lightly roasted**
   **½ teaspoon ground cinnamon**
   **several gratings of nutmeg**
   **sea salt and just-cracked pepper**
   **¼ cup olive oil**
   **¼ cup heavy cream**
   **¼ cup late-harvest white wine such as**
      **Vin Santo or Moscato**

In the work bowl of a food processor fitted with a steel blade, pulse the walnuts until they are the texture of very coarse meal (do not grind them too finely—more texture is better than less). Add the cinnamon, nutmeg, salt, and pepper, and pulse two or three more times to combine; with the machine running, pour a mixture of the olive oil, cream, and wine through the feed tube and process only until the paste is emulsified. Taste and correct the sauce for salt and spices.

*Yield:* 4 servings, as a main course

*In piú:* As divine as this sauce is, tossed with just-cooked pasta, it presents other delicious opportunities: Keep some in the refrigerator and place a spoonful over just-roasted chicken or pork; spread it on grilled bread and pass it along with cold white wine for an appetizer; enrich simple vegetable soups with a dollop, or try it as a condiment for steamed asparagus.

*Prugne Addormentate*

# Sleeping Plums

*A* serendipitous sweet born from the leftovers of a batch of bread
dough. I watched a baker up in the Friuli region throw this together as a breakfast cake for his family. The potato bread dough that serves
as its base is also delicious baked without fruit. This is a forgiving recipe,
even for the cook who does not usually make bread or dessert. Equally
wonderful made with other stone fruits (nectarines, peaches, apricots),
this sweet has become Fernando's supper of choice when he's feeling
out of sorts—not when he's actually sick with flu or a cold but more
when he's had his fill of complicated dishes (or complicated issues!) and
wants only nourishment and comfort. This was what he had for supper on
the evening after he'd given his notice at the bank. We still use the same
battered pan to bake it in, the one that's traveled with me from Saint Louis
to Venice to Tuscany.

**12 ounces potato bread dough, unrisen (see below)**
**8–10 plums, halved and stoned**
**1 cup dark brown sugar**
**3 tablespoons  cold, unsalted butter, cut into bits**
**⅔ cup heavy cream mixed with ¼ cup grappa**

Butter a round or square 9-inch cake pan and fit the dough into it; press
the plum halves, cut side up, into the dough, sprinkle over the sugar and
the butter; pour over the cream-and-grappa mixture and bake the cake at
400 degrees for 20–25 minutes or until the bread is browned, the plums
are bursting with their own juices, and the cream and sugar have formed
a golden crust.

*Yield:* 6 Servings

*Pane di Patate*
# Potato Bread

**1 pound of unpeeled baking potatoes**
**1½ small cakes fresh yeast (or 3½ teaspoons active dry yeast)**
**2 pounds all-purpose flour (about 7 cups) plus a bit extra for the**
**    kneading surface**
**1 tablespoon fine sea salt**
**1 tablespoon extra-virgin olive oil**

Boil the potatoes until tender, in sea-salted water. Drain, reserving 2 cups of the cooking water. Let water and potatoes cool down, then peel and thoroughly mash the potatoes.

Soften the yeast in a cup of lukewarm potato-cooking water for 20 minutes. In a large bowl, combine the flour, potatoes, and salt. Add the softened yeast and the remaining cup of potato water, stirring to form a dough.

Turn out the mass onto a lightly floured surface and knead to a soft, satiny, elastic texture—about 8 minutes. If the dough seems too wet, add more flour sparingly, no more than ⅓ cup. Place the dough in a clean, oiled bowl, cover with plastic wrap and a kitchen towel, and let rest and rise until doubled—about an hour. Cut the dough in half and use one piece to make *prugne addormentate* and bake the other as follows.

Gently punch down the dough, and shape a round, somewhat flat loaf. Cover with clean kitchen towels and let rise for an hour. Preheat the oven to 400 degrees. Slide the loaf onto a parchment-lined baking sheet and bake 35–40 minutes or until the crust is very brown and the bottom rings hollow when tapped. Be careful to lower the temperature slightly if the loaf is browning too quickly. Cool the loaf on a rack.

*Yield:* 2 loaves of bread or enough dough for 2 cakes. You can freeze any portion of the already risen dough; but it must be defrosted thoroughly and allowed to rise again before proceeding with either recipe.

## Fiori di Zucca Fritti
# Fried Squash Blossoms

*T*o make this simple dish all you have to do is to slip the blossoms into a silky, thin batter and then fry them in oil until they're golden. This method of preparing the tender, sweet blossoms of zucchini is the only one that respects their delicacy and the only civilized way to consume the little beauties. (Stuffing a squash blossom with ricotta or mozzarella or even an anchovy is akin to stuffing a truffle. Aside from the irreverence, the ornament couldn't possibly improve upon the blossom in its innocent state.)

This isn't a thing you'd cook for a crowd. First, because no one is ever satisfied with just a blossom or two; it's always half a dozen or more each person is hungry for, and he or she stands near the stove waiting for the next batch to brown and crisp, just like a puppy waiting for a treat. If the queue is too long, it's no fun for the cook. And second, on any given morning, it's hard to find a farmer (at least in our market) with more than a couple dozen or so blossoms he's willing to sell. So although I have made the dish for as many as four or five people, more often I fry the flowers just for Fernando and me. These and a bottle of flinty white chilled down almost to ice make our preferred lunch on a hot July afternoon.

**20 perfect zucchini blossoms**
**1 ½ cups all-purpose flour**
**beer**
**sea salt to taste**
**peanut oil**

First, with a small pair of sharp scissors, snip each petal down to the stem to open the blossom more fully. If the stems are still attached, snip them off. Sprinkle the flowers with a little water and lay them to dry, stem side up, petals spread out like a sunflower. In a shallow, broad bowl, beat together the flour and beer to form a batter that's slightly thicker than heavy cream. Stir in a little sea salt. Cover the batter and let it rest while the oil heats. Use peanut oil—a minimum depth of three inches in a heavy skillet—because it can reach the highest temperatures without smoking. Heat the oil on medium flame, as heating it too quickly results in cool spots, which result in uneven frying. When all is ready, slide the blossoms, one at a time, into the waiting oil; cook only three or four at a time. As they turn deeply golden, remove them with tongs and let sit a moment on absorbent paper. You might grind a little sea salt over them, or even better, mist them lightly with sea-salted water. When thinking about the wine, you'll want a simple white that can stand a deep chilling, for it's the icy idea of wine more than the wine itself that works so well with the just-fried, crunchy flowers.

*Yield:* 4 Servings

*Pappa al Pomodoro*
# Traditional Tuscan Tomato Porridge

*I* was never able to convince the stranger about the merits of the iced yellow tomato soup adorned with a pair of grilled, anise-perfumed prawns that I made for our first supper in the apartment. Dishes like that seemed then and seem still too precious to him. But each time I set down this traditional Tuscan porridge of fresh, ripe tomatoes stewed with yesterday's bread and wine and olive oil, he sings this childhood folksong: *"Viva la pappa col pomodoro, viva la pappa che è un capolavoro."* Freely translated it rings out: "Long live porridge with tomatoes, long live porridge that's a work of art." When I sing it to my tomato man in our market, he sings, too, always telling me how he and his brothers yearned for this dish during the long, hungry days of the Second World War.

¾ cup extra-virgin olive oil

4 fat cloves garlic, peeled, crushed, and minced

1 large yellow onion, peeled and minced

4 large, very ripe tomatoes, peeled, seeds removed, and chopped
  (or two l-pound cans of plum tomatoes, lightly crushed with
  their juices)

6 cups good beef broth, preferably homemade or 6 cups water
  (do not use chicken stock)

1 cup white wine

fine sea salt and just-cracked pepper

2 ½ cups coarse-textured, crustless bread,
  torn into ½-inch pieces

1 cup just-grated pecorino cheese (optional)

⅓ cup basil leaves, torn (not cut)

½ teaspoon good red wine vinegar

In a large soup pot, warm the olive oil and sauté the garlic and onion until they're translucent; add the tomatoes, broth or water, wine, salt, and pepper and simmer for 10 minutes. Add the bread and simmer for another 2 minutes. Remove the pot from the stove, and add the pecorino and basil, stirring to combine the elements. Let the porridge rest for at least an hour. Stir in the vinegar and serve at room temperature (or reheat to tepid or warm), in deep soup plates with a drizzle of good, green olive oil. Refrigeration absolutely destroys the porridge's pure flavor.

*Yield:* 6 servings

*Spiedini di Salsiccia e Quaglie Ripiene con Fichi sui Cuscini*

# Skewers of Sausage and Fig-Stuffed Quail Sitting on Pillows

*W*hen I saw the stranger nonchalantly licking his fingers after polishing off a lush little skewer like this one, I knew I'd chipped away at his long-standing indifference to supper.

If you're planning to serve this as picnic fare, leave the skewers intact. Allow the skewers to cool slightly; then place them in a heavy brown bag lined with branches of rosemary and leaves of sage; close the bag tightly and place it in a deep bowl to catch the juices that are bound to escape. As the quail and sausage cool, they will take on the perfume of the herbs and become even more delicious, eaten at room temperature, than they are just off the grill. Let each person deal with his or her own skewers while you pass the liver paste (see below), the wine, and napkins.

- 12 **farm-raised quail, cleaned, rinsed, dried, salted and peppered, and stuffed with several leaves of fresh sage, a few rosemary leaves, and half a fresh black or green fig (reserve the livers for paste)**
- 12 **thin slices of pancetta**
- 12 **2-inch slices of fennel-scented sausage (or other Italian-style, sweet sausage) poached for 5 minutes in simmering water and drained**
- 12 **1-inch-thick slices of coarse-textured bread**
- ½ **cup white wine**
- 2 **tablespoons unsalted butter**
- 2 **shallots, peeled and minced**
- **the reserved quail livers plus 3 ounces chicken livers, trimmed and chopped**
- 2 **tablespoons Vin Santo or other sweet wine**
- ½ **teaspoon ground allspice**
- **sea salt and just-cracked pepper**

Wrap each quail in a slice of pancetta, securing it with a wooden pick; thread the quail onto 6 skewers, alternating with slices of bread and sausage. Grill the skewers in the oven over a pan to catch their drippings; baste with white wine, giving each skewer a quarter turn every 3–4 minutes. Continue the basting and rotating until the quail are golden and the sausage crisp (18–20 minutes in all). Meanwhile warm the butter in a small pan and sauté the shallots until translucent; add the chopped livers and sauté for 3 minutes until they are colored outside but still pink inside; add the Vin Santo, allspice, salt, and pepper and sauté another minute, mashing the mixture to a coarse paste. (This paste can be made in greater quantities, using all chicken livers or a combination of the livers of chicken, quail, pheasant, and duck with proportionately increased measures of butter, shallot, Vin Santo, and allspice. It is nice to have ready to spread on thin slices of just-toasted bread to serve with *aperitivi*.) When the *spiedini* are cooked, let your guests slide the meats off their skewers onto warmed plates, spread the grilled bread with some of the liver paste, and sit each quail on its bread "pillow."

*Yield:* 6 servings

❧

*Zucca al Forno Ripiena con Porcini e Tartufi*

# Whole Roasted Pumpkin Stuffed with Porcini and Truffles

*I*f the stranger had let me cook for our wedding, I would have brought forth this roasted pumpkin as a first course. The natural sugars in the pumpkin caramelize and melt into the cheeses, while the truffles perfume the whole luscious mass, all of it sending up wonderfully sensual aromas. Even without the truffles, this is spectacular. If there's one dish to add to your repertoire, this is it. Actually it's a repertoire in itself.

1 large pumpkin or Hubbard squash, approximately 4–5 pounds
in weight, its stalk end cut around to form a cap, seeds and
strings removed from the cavity (retain stalk end for later)

3 tablespoons unsalted butter

2 large yellow onions, peeled and minced

12 ounces fresh wild mushrooms (porcini, cèpes, chanterelles,
portobelli) rinsed, drained, dried, and sliced thinly (or 4 ounces
dried porcini, softened in ½ cup warm water, stock, or wine,
drained, and sliced thinly)

2 whole black diamond truffles from Norcia (or 2 canned black
truffles or 3 ounces black truffle paste), optional

sea salt

1 teaspoon just-cracked white pepper

3 cups mascarpone

12 ounces Emmenthaler cheese, grated

4 ounces Parmesan cheese, grated

3 whole eggs, beaten

2 teaspoons just-grated nutmeg

4 tablespoons unsalted butter

8 slices firm-textured, day-old white bread,
crusts removed, cut into 1-inch squares

In a medium sauté pan, melt the butter and sauté the onion with the
mushrooms until both soften and the mushrooms give up their their liquors
(if using dried mushrooms, strain the soaking liquid and add it to the sauté
pan). Add the thinly sliced truffles or the truffle paste (if used) and combine
well. Add the salt and pepper. In a large bowl, combine all the remaining
ingredients except the bread and butter; season with liberal amounts of salt
and pepper. Beat until well combined, then stir in the mushrooms, onions,
and truffles. Melt the 4 tablespoons of butter in a sauté pan and brown the
bread, tossing the pieces about until they are crisp. Place the pumpkin or

squash in a large, heavy baking dish or on a baking sheet. Spoon one-third of the mushroom mixture into the pumpkin, add half the crisped bread, another third of the mushrooms, and the remaining bread, ending with the mushrooms. Top off with the pumpkin cap and roast at 375 degrees for 1½ hours or until the pumpkin's flesh is very soft. Carry the pumpkin immediately to table, remove its hat, and spoon out portions of its flesh with the stuffing. The dish needs only a cool, flinty, dry white wine as accompaniment.

*Yield:* 8 to 10 servings

*Vitello Brasato con Uve del Vino*

# Loin of Veal Braised with Wine Grapes

*A*nd this would have been the main course at our wedding lunch if *I'd* been cooking. A beautiful autumn dish full of color and surprise— the grapes plump and softened in the wine and the warm tartness of the fruit against the sweetness of the veal make for a fine marriage. If you're not serving the pumpkin or any other substantial first course, serve this over garlic mashed potatoes. Change the veal to pork and the white wine to red wine. and you'll have a heartier set of flavors.

**12 veal tenderloins (about 4 ounces each)**
**1 teaspoon fine sea salt**
**3 tablespoons fresh rosemary leaves, finely minced**
**10 whole cloves of garlic, crushed**
**6 tablespoons unsalted butter**
**1 tablespoon extra-virgin olive oil**
**1½ cups dry white wine**
**3 cups white or purple wine grapes (or table grapes)**
**1 tablespoon 12-year-old balsamic vinegar**

Wipe the veal with paper towels and rub its surfaces with salt, rosemary, and crushed cloves. Heat oil and 4 tablespoons of butter over medium flame in a large sauté pan. When the butter begins to foam, add the tenderloins (only the number that fits comfortably in the pan without crowding). Sauté until golden on all sides, removing them to a holding plate while you cook the remaining ones. Rinse the sauté pan with the wine, scraping up any bits, and let the wine reduce for five minutes. Add the grapes and the browned veal to the pan and lower the flame so that the wine barely simmers. Gently braise the veal for 4 to 5 minutes or until the flesh begins to feel firm when you prod it with a finger. Don't overcook the veal. Remove the veal to a platter, covering it very loosely so as not to "steam" it, and let it rest. Raise the flame and reduce the braising liquids once again, until they begin to thicken. Remove from the flame, add the remaining 2 tablespoons of butter and the balsamic vinegar. Stir well and pour the sauce over the veal. Don't worry about the grape seeds or, if you must worry, America is full of the seedless ones.

*Yield:* 8 servings

*Porcini Brasati con Moscato*

# Wild Mushrooms Braised in Late-Harvest Wine

O f all the dishes we cooked during our sojourn at the hotel next door to our apartment during the renovation, this one has earned the status of family treasure. We cook it anytime and everywhere we can barter, hunt, buy, or beg a basketful of porcini. After successful autumn hunts, we make a dose big enough to feed the neighbors, and we stage our own Sagra di Porcini.

5 tablespoons unsalted butter

1 tablespoon extra-virgin olive oil

1 pound of fresh wild mushrooms (porcini, cèpes, chanterelles, portobelli), wiped free of surface grit with a soft, damp cloth and thinly sliced

½ pound shallots, peeled and minced

fine sea salt and just-cracked pepper

1 cup Moscato or other late-harvest white wine

1 cup heavy cream

4–5 fresh sage leaves

Over medium flame, warm 3 tablespoons of butter with the olive oil in a large sauté pan and, when the butter foams, add the mushrooms and the shallots, tossing them about to coat them in the hot fat. Lower the flame and sauté until the mushrooms begin to give up their juices. Sprinkle salt and pepper generously over all. Add the wine and continue to braise gently for 20 minutes, until almost all the wine and the exuded juices have been absorbed by the mushrooms. Meanwhile, in a small saucepan over low flame, warm the heavy cream with the leaves of sage. When the mixture is close to simmering, remove from the stove and cover (the cream will take on the perfume of the sage while the mushrooms braise). Strain the cream and discard the sage. Now add the perfumed cream to the mushrooms and continue the very slow braise, permitting the cream to reduce for 2 or 3 minutes. Serve the dish very warm with thin toast and glasses of the same chilled Moscato used in the braise.

*Yield:* 4 servings

*Sgroppino*

# Lemon Gelato with Vodka and Sparkling Wine

*I* learned quickly to love this icy, creamy, addictive ending to nearly every lunch or dinner served in every *osteria* and *ristorante* across the Veneto. Alas, no one even knows what *sgroppino* is here in the Umbrian hills, where we now live. Though I never made the drink at home in Venice, after we moved I began to improvise it from sheer nostalgia. It is so light and goes down so easily, one feels almost noble about drinking it—as though one has forsaken dessert and settled for a cool drink. Here is our house version.

½ **pint lemon ice cream or sherbert**
4–6 **ice cubes**
4 **ounces vodka**
1 **cup sparkling wine (in the Veneto, it's the ever present Prosecco)**
**shredded zest of 1 lemon**

Place the ice cream or sherbert, the ice, vodka, and wine in a blender and whirl until it's thick, creamy, and barely pourable. Transfer it to iced wineglasses, sprinkle on the lemon zest, and serve with small spoons.

## *Acknowledgments*

*I*t was Sue Pollock who took me by the hand, saying, "First we have to find you the most wonderful agent."

And Sue brought me straight to Rosalie Siegel who, like all magical people are wont to do, changed the course of my life. Rosalie is Jeanne d'Arc in a Chanel suit. She is a sage. Tenaciously, devotedly, and with that rare finesse of hers, she shepherded me and my story. Now I can't imagine any story of mine without her.

From across six thousand miles of land and sea, Amy Gash reined me in. No less than a brilliant editor, she saved me from an excess of "floating, hovering, lunging, festooning, raising up, and dancing." She helped me to lay down some old trappings, to stand up taller as a writer. Anyone who still thinks that editing is all about punctuation and grammar should know the depth of her work. Amy loved this story and cared, unstintingly, how I told it. And everywhere in this text that three adjectives remain still lined up in a row is a result of my stubbornness, a sign of the skirmish or two among our battles that Amy let me win.

This book was made by every Venetian who showed me the way or told me a secret, every one of you who sipped Prosecco with me, taught me a word, fed me, hugged me, rescued me. And cried with me. You are a race apart, a tribe more blessed than cursed and that I lived among you for those thousand days is a divine keepsake, one that burnishes even the thinnest blaze of the sun and keeps me warm.

Finally, it's not that I don't remember you, you about whom I did not write among these pages. It's not even that I don't remember you kindly or not so kindly, as the case may be. But this is such a small book and my life is such a long story that this is all I can say for now.

# A Thousand Days in Venice

How to Fall in Love in Venice

Addresses to Remember

# How to Fall in Love in Venice

1. If you can, be in Venice on the third Saturday of July. La Festa del Redentore is the most genuinely Venetian festival on the calendar. In it the Venetians gives thanks to the Redeemer (il Redentore) for delivering their ancestors from the plague in 1575. When you book your lodgings, ask the hotel to book seats for dinner on one of the larger boats plying the canal that evening or, better yet and only if you're adventurous, to rent a *sandolo,* a small traditional rowboat for you. Staying on shore as a spectator—rather than being in the midst of the festival on the water—is lovely only if you're the guest of a host whose *palazzo* has a rooftop terrace from which vantage you can see and feel the spectacle. Even that, though, isn't quite as glorious as floating among the candelit boats under the moonlight to the sound of the mandolins, passing wine bottles and plates of *sarde in soar* (fried sardines served with caramelized onions, raisins, and pine nuts, a dish with Arabic origins dating back to La Serenissima) back and forth with the boats next door. Everything quietens at 11:00 P.M. when the fireworks begin, and then, at midnight, the eating and drinking part of the festival recommences.

2. Fill a sack or a basket with bread and *zaletti* (cornmeal cookies) from Colussi, a bakery in San Marco; cheese and cold meats from

any one of the no-name shops gracing every Venetian neighborhood; wine, pastry, and chocolates from Rosasalva—and take the vaporetto (water taxi) to the Lido where you can board the number eleven bus for *i murazzi,* the immense rock wall that protects the island from the sea. Walk a hundred meters, find a flat rock on which to spread your meal, and then dine to the accompaniment of crashing Adriatic waves.

3. At *crepuscolo* (dusk) head for the terrace bar at the Hotel Monaco, housed in the seventeenth-century palazzo of the noble Vallaresso family. It looks out on a particularly glorious section of the Grand Canal, proving that the Venice of one's dreams is the real Venice. Best to tell the barman to concoct his own special *aperitivo* for you. Just say, *"Ci pensi lei.* You decide."

4. Stroll in the Dorsoduro, the Venice neighborhood that some have likened to Paris's Left Bank. Tucked here and there you'll find boutiques, cafés, and restaurants. Begin at Venice's only wooden bridge, the Accademia, constructed in 1932 to replace the great iron monstrosity built by the Austrians during their mid-nineteenth-century reign. Along the way, you might be inspired to renew your marriage vows at La Basilica di Santa Maria della Salute. Afterward, secure a table in the jasmine-scented gardens at Locanda Montin: start your meal with *canoce,* thin, sweet shanks of Adriatic shellfish; next consider a silky *risotto alla zucca* (risotto with pumpkin), or try the roasted lagoon duck stuffed with local sausages and wild herbs. And when you've emptied that bottle of Bianco di Custoza, crisp white wine from the nearby village of Bussolengo, call for *due sgroppini,* the clas-

sic close to all Venetian suppers. What will soon appear are two flutes filled with lemon sorbet, vodka, and sparkling wine whipped to a thick, icy cream.

5. Go early, about 7:00 A.M., to the Rialto markets and watch the "getting ready" drama. Then follow the farmers and merchants to their favorite bars for cappuccino and hot *cornetti* filled with apricot jam. Walk back through the open-air stalls of cheeses, fruits, vegetables, and meats as more shoppers begin to arrive, and by 9:30 A.M. make your first stop at Cantina do Mori, the oldest wine bar in Venice, where the extraordinary circumstances of your visit might make it possible to drink a glass of simple wine from the barrel along with *panini ripieni con prosciutto crudo e uove sode* (crisp buns stuffed with cured ham and hard-cooked eggs), just as all the farmers and fishermen are doing.

6. Pack a blanket and head for the nearby island of Torcello. Take the *motonave* (ferry boat) from Lido, preferably the one that departs at 8:20 A.M., and sit outside sipping the cappuccino you picked up at Chizzolin on the Grand Viale. On Torcello spread your blanket in the tall grasses on either side of the main path and just stay quiet, feeling the ancient stillness of the place. When you're ready to move, visit the bedizened basilica, the site on which the original seventh-century church was erected, and then head to Ponte del Diavolo (Bridge of the Devil) for lunch. Ask for a table where the waiter with the salmon-colored cravat and the pomaded hair parted in the middle can take care of you. If it's May, don't forget to order *risotto con i bruscandoli* (risotto with hop shoots).

7. Go late, after supper in the summer, to sit outdoors at Florian, sipping cold Moscato—sweet, amber-colored wine—and listen to the orchestra. Dance to the last piece of the evening and have a nightcap with the musicians before you and your companion wander back home.

8. Watch the sunset on the vaporetto number one. Board the boat at the San Zaccaria landing stage just as the light is beginning to change and settle on one of the benches out on the deck. Open an iced bottle of Prosecco (paper cups are permissible but a pair of Murano flutes, which you'll take back as souveniers, would be better). Hopefully there'll be a breeze. The light will change as you glide down the most beautiful street on the planet. Debark at Santa Lucia and reboard a number one heading back toward the center of Venice. The Prosecco will be finished, and you'll be starving by the time you reach the Ca' d'Oro stop. But La Vedova waits only a few meters away off the Strada Nuova. Step inside and step back a century, maybe two. Squeeze into the crowd of locals at the little *banco* who'll be downing *ombrette* (small tumblers of white wine) and calling for *cichetti* (something to munch out of hand). La Vedova is revered by the Venetians, adored by travelers. Nothing here is tarted up for tourists, because since each dish on the menu is a faithful reproduction of the traditional *cucina Veneziana*. If you've not been invited to supper in a Venetian home, La Vedova is the next best option. Please give Mirella and Renzo a hug from me.

# Addresses to Remember

## Bacari

*Cantina do Mori*
San Polo 429—Rialto
Phone 041 5225401
Closed Sunday and Wednesday

*La Mascareta*
Castello 5183
Calle Lunga Santa Maria Formosa
Phone 041 5230744
Closed Sunday

## Traditional Osterie-Ristoranti

*Ca' D'Oro (La Vedova)*
Cannaregio 3912
Ramo Ca' d'Oro
Phone 041 5285324
Closed Thursday

*Al Mascaron*
Castello 5225
Calle Lunga Santa Maria Formosa
Phone 041 5225995
Closed Sunday

*Vini da Gigio*
Cannaregio 3628A
Fondamenta San Felice
Phone 041 5285140
Website www.vinidagigio.com
E-Mail info@vinidagigio.com
Closed Monday

*Fiaschetteria Toscana*
Cannaregio 5719
Fondamenta San Giovanni
   Crisostomo
Phone 041 5285281
Website www.fiaschetteria
   toscana.it
Closed Tuesday

*Harry's Bar*
San Marco 1323
Calle Vallaresso
Phone 041 5285777
Website www.cipriani.com
Never closed

## Bar e Pasticcerie

*Rosasalva*
San Marco
Mercerie San Salvador
Phone 041 5227934
Website www.rosasalva.it
Closed Sunday

*Caffè Florian*
Piazza San Marco
Phone 041 5205641
Website www.caffeflorian.com
E-Mail info@caffeflorian.com
Closed Wednesday

## Where to Shop

*Mario Bevilacqua*
San Marco 2520
Campo Santa Maria del Giglio
Phone 041 2410662
Website www.bevilacquatessuti.com
Email info@bevilacquatessuti.com

Woven silks, brocade, damasks, and velvets from ancient Venetian
designs have been fashioned on the wooden looms of the noble family

of Bevilacqua for more than two hundred years. In addition, many of these fabrics have been transformed into decorative pillows, table runners, and wall hangings

*Papier-Mâché*
Castello 5175
Calle Lunga Santa Maria Formosa
Phone 041 5229995
Website www.papiermache.com

Hand-crafted and painted papier-mâché carnival masks in traditional designs.

*Maurizio Sumiti*
Castello 5274
Calle delle Bande
Phone and fax 041 5205621

Handmade reproductions of Venetian decorative objects in gold-rubbed wood and metal

*Missiaglia*
San Marco 125-127
Piazza San Marco
Phone 041 5224464
Website www.missiaglia.com

Jewelers to the nobility since 1846. The hand-made sterling silver pepper grinder in the form of an artichoke is a signature gift item.

*Venetia Studium*
San Marco 2403
Via XXII Marzo
Phone 041 5229281
Website www.fortunylamps.com

Silk and silk velvet purses, scarves, dresses, and decorative objects for the home, inspired by the designs of Mariano Fortuny.

*Giuliana Longo*
San Marco 4813
Calle dell'Ovo
Phone 041 5226454

Hats for men and women.

## Small Hotels

*Locanda Novo*
Cannaregio 4529
Calle dei Preti
Phone 041 2411496
Website www.locandanovo.it

*Casa Querini*
Castello 4388
Campo San Giovanni Novo
Phone 041 2411294
Website www.locandaquerini.com

*Casa de Uscoli*
San Marco 2818
Phone 041 2410669
Website www.casauscoli.com

*Cà Valeri*
Castello 3845
Ramo dei Corazzieri
Phone 041 2411530
Website www.locandacavaleri.com

*Locanda Armizo*
San Polo 1104
Campo San Silvestro
Phone 041 5206473
Website www.locandaarmizo.com

# About the Author

An American chef and food and wine journalist, Marlena de Blasi has written five memoirs, a novel, and two books about the regional foods of Italy. She lives with her husband in the Umbrian hill town of Orvieto. Her work has been translated into twenty-six languages.

Join us at **AlgonquinBooksBlog.com** for the latest news on all of our stellar titles, including weekly giveaways, behind-the-scenes snapshots, book and author updates, original videos, media praise, detailed tour information, and other exclusive material.

You'll also find information about the **Algonquin Book Club**, a selection of the perfect books—from award winners to international bestsellers—to stimulate engaging and lively discussion. Helpful book group materials are available, including

**Book excerpts**
**Downloadable discussion guides**
**Author interviews**
**Original author essays**
**Book club tips and ideas**
**Wine and recipe pairings**

**twitter** **Follow us on twitter.com/AlgonquinBooks**
**facebook** **Become a fan on facebook.com/AlgonquinBooks**